A SURVIVAL GUIDE FOR NEWSPAPERS

News *by* Design

ROBERT LOCKWOOD

QUARK
PRESS

Library of Congress Catalog Card Number 91–061823
ISBN 0–926432–00–1

Printed in the United States of America

Published in 1992 by Quark Press.
Denver, Colorado, U.S.A.

Library of Congress Cataloging-in-Publication Data

Lockwood, Robert, 1936-
  News by Design: A Survival Guide for Newspapers

A Quark Press publication

To Nancy, Jaime-Pilar and Helen

A metaphor for life itself

In three dimensions

ROBERT should have written this book 30 years ago, so that the generations of today's newspaper designers would have grown up benefiting from his wisdom and thoughtfulness while working to reshape newspapers. I, for one, regret not having been able to read it sooner, although I've benefited personally for more than a dozen years from Robert's insights into how people communicate — both in two dimensions (on paper) and in three dimensions (human to human). The moments we've shared together discussing the relationship between the human condition and the newspaper condition are now finally captured for posterity; all his pearls of verbal wisdom are now in book form. (Perhaps I should have taken notes over all those dinners we've shared.)

This is a book I'll ask my children to read, regardless of the career paths they choose, for it speaks directly to the challenge of not stereotyping people into "word people" or "visual people," or any other sorts of stereotypes. I would hope that their friend Robert's book would challenge them to think in new and better ways, to change the world in their own manner, and not to rely on doing anything "because it's always been done that way." This is a lot to ask of a book written ostensibly about newspaper design. But Robert never has spoken directly of that discipline, instead seeing newspaper design as a metaphor for life itself.

by Richard Curtis
Managing Editor,
Graphics & Photography
USA TODAY

Designing newspapers
Creating chaos out of order

IF someone ever says to you, "I think we need to redesign our newspaper," your first reply should be, "O.K., but first we have to redesign the publisher." Publishers are the true designers of newspapers because they create the organizational culture, the managerial climate — and they control the purse strings.

The biggest obstacle to redesigning a newspaper is the human and institutional resistance to change. Most newspapers are rigid, stratified organizations bound by rules and procedures that have worked in the past but may no longer be useful as guides to the future. From the structure of the organization you can predict the energy and excitement of the newspaper itself. Any concept of newspaper design should include an examination of the organization and newsroom operation.

Eventually, all organizations require renewal and revitalization. Orderly and predictable people get used to how things work and create barriers to change so they can get on with their business without too much fuss. Keeping things the way they have always been becomes comforting. People approach tasks with fixed attitudes, "mental templates" of how things ought to fit and function. "Because we've always done it that way" becomes a refrain against new ideas and approaches. Reactive thinking replaces critical and creative thinking. And so it is at many newspapers.

Change is easier for those who initiate it than for those who are affected by it but have no say in it. Change destroys the old ways of doing things by breaking things apart, questioning and analyzing everything and putting things together in a different way. In a sense, it creates chaos out of the existing order. Move a chair in a newsroom and someone's career is threatened. Advance the idea that photographs and graphics can also communicate, and reporters are threatened and accuse you of betraying the word.

There has been a curious development in newsrooms in recent years. The word "word" has taken on a kind of mystical fogginess.

People use it as a symbol, representing the one true canon of journalism that sets up barriers to any change in the newspaper. It's used as an icon, disconnected from any context or regard for syntax, clarity of expression or objective writing and a graceful style. The word "word" by itself is not much use as a tool for thought in any discussion on communication. "Not enough words on the page," someone says of a design prototype, sounding like Emperor Joseph II of Austria in the motion picture *Amadeus* when he comments to Mozart on a new composition: "Too many notes."

Although newspapers are a totally visual form of communication, we somehow take for granted the separation of image and words. In print journalism image and word are indivisibly wed. The medium makes the narrative come alive in a special way — readers remember the message through the form.

Print journalists mostly trained in "verbal" skills have not refined their "visual" skills. As a result, many newspapers tend to be a mass of gray "content" decorated with some "art." Only when we realize that content is art and what is written cannot be separated from how it's written can we begin to connect with readers more effectively.

In this book I intend to show that the path to better newspapers begins with (1) recognizing the diversity and complexity of the world we are reporting and explaining and (2) understanding that the closed management systems we created in the past are inadequate to the challenges of the future. It's essential that we redesign our newspapers, our newsrooms, ourselves.

The definition of design used in this book is broadened to include not only an ability to manipulate type and understand publishing strategies, editorial requirements, space planning (traditional design skills), but also the ability to find and offer solutions for redesigning the organizational structure and the managerial climate of the newspaper.

Also, I have tried to demonstrate the link between the way we organize people and the resulting product: that it's only through the intelligence, imagination and energy of individuals that newspapers become alive, charged with energy and vitality.

The newspaper design process creates chaos out of order to discover a new order. And when you look for order you find beauty.

R.L.

"Where is the life we have lost in living? Where is the wisdom we have lost in knowledge? Where is the knowledge we have lost in information?"
T.S. Eliot

MANY people have helped in the production and writing of this book. The case studies were written by editors involved in the projects at their newspapers. Others have contributed through their ideas on journalism and design, their suggestions and their friendship.

Ed Miller, with whom I began my journalism career, wrote the case study on *The Morning Call* of Allentown, Pa., and collaborated with me on ideas that were incorporated in the section, "Art of Change." I worked with Craig Ammerman on the redesign of *The Philadelphia Bulletin* and later on an experimental prototype for the *Los Angeles Herald.* He reports on both design efforts. Jim Willse wrote the case study for the New York *Daily News.* He was managing editor of the paper in 1985 when he invited me to meet with him, then-editor Gil Spencer and publisher Jim Hoge to discuss ideas for a redesign. In 1986 I began work on three newspapers in Italy. Andrea Franchini headed the design team on the project and wrote the case study for the process that led to the redesign of *Il Resto del Carlino, La Nazione* and *Il Piccolo.* The Colorado Springs *Gazette Telegraph* design team was chaired by John Hutchinson, assistant managing editor in charge of graphics and photography, who produced the piece on the redesign of that paper. The last study, on *The London* (Ontario) *Free Press* by editor Phil McLeod, completes the section on case studies. It also completes a cycle that began with Ed Miller's goal in 1978 to reinvent the newspaper for the 1980s and ends with Phil McLeod's ambition in 1988 to reinvent the newspaper for the 1990s.

I also want to acknowledge those whose work, ideas and friendships have helped shape my ideas and influenced my work. I am particularly indebted to Edwin Taylor and Ed Miller for our shared views in the possibilities of the discipline; to Nigel Holmes and Walter Bernard for setting an example for all designers by their strength of character and beautiful work; to Fred Ebrahimi whose vision of technology and design is that it should serve to better the human condition; to Nancy McCarthy at Quark for her help guiding the book through to completion; and to Gene Giancarlo for his contribution to journalism through the American Society of Newspaper Editors and for his careful attention to style in this book.

As with all of my projects, nothing much would have been accomplished without the sound advice and help from my wife, friend and editor — thank you, Nancy. ❦

Credits
Editors:
Gene Giancarlo
Nancy B. Lockwood
Production assistance:
Michael Leary
Illustrations pages 32 to 35, page 115: Nigel Holmes
Additional illustrations:
Michael Leary
Layout software:
QuarkXPress
Reproduction:
Crosfield Electronics

☛ **Note**: *The icon* ◉ *is used throughout the book to signify* see page.

by **Robert Lockwood**

Robert Lockwood's first newspaper design was *The Morning Call*, in Allentown, Pa. Previously, he taught design at the Philadelphia College of Art.

He is a cofounder and first president of the Society of Newspaper Design.

Lockwood offers editorial design and development consulting services to newspapers worldwide through his company, Robert Lockwood, Inc. Since 1980 he has designed more than 50 newspapers.

Many of his redesign projects involve newsroom restructuring, the introduction of PC and Macintosh technology, and strategic planning on an organizational level.

In addition, since 1984, he has worked with the Associated Press to enhance its graphics report to members.

Lockwood holds bachelor's and master's degrees in fine art from the Tyler School of Art, Temple University.

Section one

Visual thinking

Seeing in a new way

Visual thinking

Seeing in a new way

Human beings invented narrative to give the illusion of order. The pictograph — a picture representing an object such as a goat or a horse — was the first attempt at recording ideas. For centuries, in Jacob Bronowski's phrase, "The hand was the cutting edge of the mind." Ideas, expressed through language and images, were drawn or carved. The technology was simple. One of the world's first recorded stories, *Gilgamesh*, was written on clay tablets using a six-column (sound familiar?) format. Signs and symbols were united in dynamic organization. Originally, people considered words to be "momentary deities" or epiphanies. Writing and letterforms evolved to change all that. With the abstraction of writing, pictographs no longer retained their original meanings. They became a coded language to be taught and learned. Images were separated from words, creating — in effect — two distinct languages. This led to a form of specialization that exists today. It's not uncommon to have someone you've just met in a newsroom say, "Hi, I'm a word person." (I'm always tempted to respond, "Which word?")

The invention of movable type by Johann Gutenberg about A.D. 1450 increased our dependency on linear thinking with its stress on one-at-a-timeness over the more inclusive all-at-onceness of visual thinking. The Renaissance saw single-point perspective replace the mosaic. Literate man began to live in what James Joyce called "ABCED-mindedness." As a result of this "fragmenting of the field of perception and the breaking of movement into static bits," says Edmund Carpenter, "man won a power of applied knowledge and technology unrivaled in human history. The price he paid was existing personally and socially in a state of almost total subliminal awareness."

The way we see things, to a degree, is conditioned by our technologies. The mechanical age with its habit of dealing with things in fragmented bits has made it difficult for people to function in the new electronic world of bits *and* bytes. Hardwired somewhere deep in our brains are A to B to C templates. We are in the grip of a mechanical and fragmentary view of the world. We've adapted to the conventional structure of mechanistic thinking and have assumed the values of that structure. Perhaps that's why the transition from the mechanical to the electronic age is so traumatic. We need to reconfigure the templates so we can think and, thereby, see verbally *and* visually.

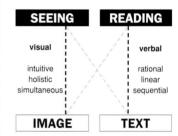

"Seeing and reading are two modes through which we traditionally think of receiving messages. Image and text are two carriers of those messages. Typically we think of seeing as a visual process connected with images — we see the landscape, we see a painting. This process is intuitive, emotional, and simultaneous, experienced almost involuntarily … . On the other hand, the process of reading is typically connected with the verbal process of decoding text's written language signs — letters. To do this one must know the code. One must have learned to read the particular language of the message. This process is cerebral, rational, deliberate, and linear."

Katherine McCoy

from *Design Quarterly 148*

Detail of the Column of Marcus Aurelius

**With no point of view ascribed, the viewer can begin and end anywhere. The choreography
of the reliefs moves the viewer smoothly through the story and helps make the narrative
come alive.**

Piazza di Colonna

**Through the organizing
strength of the vertical line
we can visualize and
understand the composition
of the column in its totality
and see it in its relationship
to the surrounding square.**

A news column by any other name.

The Roman newspaper *Il Tempo* is situated in an ancient palazzo in the
center of the city between two beautiful piazzas, the Piazza di Colonna
in front and the Piazza di Montecitorio to the rear. In the center of each
piazza, and dominating it, is a vertical signpost — a Roman column in
the Piazza di Colonna and an Egyptian obelisk in the Piazza di
Montecitorio. The contrast is remarkable.

Facing *Il Tempo* is the column of Marcus Aurelius, A.D. 190, which
gives the Piazza di Colonna its name. The column tells the news of
Marcus Aurelius's campaigns against the Marcomanni and other
Germanic tribes. It's an early example of presenting news graphically,
but without today's computer-aided design programs this "one-column"
information graphic took about a year to complete. We "read" the
column from bottom to top. The carved reliefs weave a seamless spiral
describing events in the campaign as they unfolded in time. The narrative
style is naturalistic, with a clear beginning, middle, and end. And, as with
all good visual sequences, an interesting rhythm is struck. Because you
must walk around the column to read it, the story unfolds thematically, as
in a well-designed news package (◉ 111, 117).

The technology, the act of chiseling, shaped both the narrative of
the column and the Roman letterforms at its base. The text face you're
reading (with its chiseled serifs) is derived from such Roman writing.

Detail of the obelisk
The incised relief acts as a light-catcher, creating on one side a line of shadow and on the other light.

Piazza di Montecitorio
The vertical obelisk is the central axis to which all other points in the square relate.

To the west, adjoining the Piazza di Colonna, is the Piazza di Montecitorio. In the center of the piazza, facing the Parliament Building, stands an Egyptian obelisk from the sixth century B.C. The juxtaposition of the column and the obelisk highlights two aspects of visual thinking: the naturalistic and the symbolic. The obelisk differs from the column in both message and form. Its symbols have the solemn authority of holy signs or computer chips. They are nonlinear and grasped by the eye all at once. The column is substance carved into physical shapes or reliefs that can be understood as tangible objects; the obelisk is incised with abstract symbols that can be seen as containers of energy. Just as the images of electronic circuitry and telecommunications portray a new world of complex processes, early societies portrayed complex processes through symbols.

Situated between the two columns, *Il Tempo* is emblematic of the drama of contemporary society: the transition to an electronic technology from a mechanical one. It is caught between two ways of seeing and thinking. From the advantage of our modern perspective, we can look on both past and present technologies, choose between different ways of seeing and thinking, and use whichever works without being bound by either one. In an age when information retrieval is both instant and total, journalists at *Il Tempo* and elsewhere are learning to think visually.

Word images
Obelisks, unlike the Roman column, are read from the top down and are described by Pliny the Elder as "petrified rays of sunlight." The symbols, incised on the flat face of the granite to withstand the grinding forces of desert sandstorms, stand alone — each symbol a word, each word an image.
R.L.

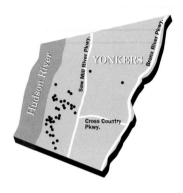

A detective graphic

This dot map of subsidized housing shows how a graphic presentation of information can reveal patterns that would be hidden if the same information were presented as a statistical list. A judge accused Yonkers city officials of a "pattern and practice of racial discrimination." The dots show that subsidized housing was largely in the nonwhite western part of Yonkers.

R.L.

Thinking visually suggests seeing in a new way. It emphasizes associative thinking and the recognition of patterns — in thoughts or dots. It can be applied to a graphic, such as the map at left, a story, a news page, the total newspaper, or even economic patterns and readership trends. With a news story it can mean, for example, thinking about the shape of the information, not only its length. It may involve analyzing the information and synthesizing it in a way that makes sense for the reader. By looking at a story in this way an editor may decide that a narrative handling may not be the most appropriate form. Day Five of a gas crisis, for example, may need a different approach. The reader doesn't need a story here — he already knows there's a shortage. A map showing which stations are closed and, more important, which are open, may be more useful (48). The results of editors "seeing" information this way are pages in which content determines the shape of the story and the look of the page. The news is allowed to assert itself in a visually interesting way.

The entire newspaper can be visually represented, showing not only news and advertising columns but also the best shapes for each. Drawing a flat plan makes the architecture of a section apparent, and helps editors find ways to enhance the shapes and create an interesting rhythm and pacing throughout (24).

Some disciplines emphasize visual thinking more than others, and print journalism is one of them. Visual thinking, a human faculty each of us possesses, is strengthened with practice. In the next several pages are examples of work from print journalists whose job is to think and present information visually.

TᑌNNEL vision

Above is an example of visual thinking in Ivan Chermayeff's play on the word "tunnel."

Columbia, Mo.

Good ideas don't require big bucks, as seen in this coverage of local elections in the *Columbia* (Mo.) *Daily Tribune* in 1979. "We often had brainstorming sessions: anywhere between five to ten writers, editors, and photographers," explains Bill Marr, who was picture and graphics editor then. "No ideas were too ridiculous: All were considered in a somewhat noncompetitive atmosphere. The dynamics of the *Tribune* of the mid- to late 1970s under managing editor Carolyn White happened not just from the talents of those involved, but from a rare collection of personalities that fit together — a fit in a work environment which I have not experienced since."

On Day One of the election coverage, the *Tribune* ran a photo lineup (by Nick Kelsh, photographer for the series) of all the candidates across the top of the front and back pages, thus creating a strong graphic image. On subsequent days individual candidates were featured in greater detail. The photo image is retained by outlining the candidates not featured and throwing them into the background while highlighting the ones featured. The approach is original and adds a human touch to election coverage, which is frequently done in a dry, statistical manner.

Bill Marr:

Creating a strong photographic image

Process

We need to reorganize visual habits so that "things" are not perceived as isolated in space but as having structure, order, and relatedness to both space and time.

R.L.

Randy Stano:
Showing and telling all sides of the story

"A road sign indicating a right curve is more effective than a marker merely spelling out 'Right Curve.' The graphic sign stimulates visual thinking. The driver 'sees' the coming curve ahead and adjusts to it. A word sign appeals to his intellectual thinking. He has to interpret the meaning of the words before he can adjust his actions."
Rudolf Modley
from *Sign Image Symbol*, edited by *Gyorgy Kepes*

The Miami Herald

It was Jan. 16, 1989, and William E. Lozano, a Miami police officer, was charged with the fatal shooting of a motorcyclist, Clement Lloyd, and the related death of his passenger, Allan Blanchard.

The trial threatened to tear Miami apart once again. The idea to diagram the incident in order to show how several witnesses saw it emerged during a news meeting.

Randy Stano describes the process: "We had to make sense of a stack of depositions 10 inches high. Jackson Dykman, assistant graphics editor, dissected the information for the graphic. Reggie Myers, the artist, and Dykman, accompanied by a photographer, visited the scene of the shooting in Miami's Overtown section. The photographer took pictures of the street and the buildings while Myers made sketches. Dykman verified the position of trees, buildings, fire hydrants and other landmarks from a police diagram, and he and Myers put together the basic design for the graphic."

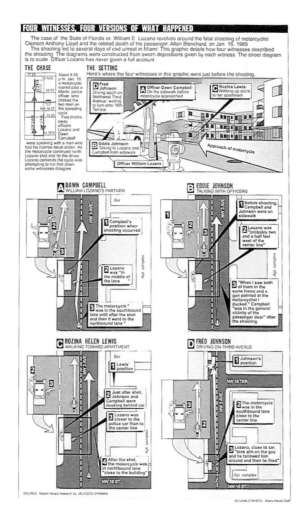

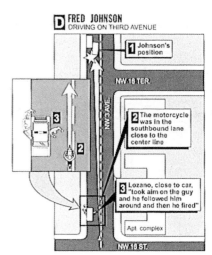

Mario Garcia:
Measuring success with a grid

Contrast
Dynamic tension through the use of contrast can be achieved in many ways, as seen on the page at left. On an esthetic level Emmett Courant *graphics director Jan Van Keoter uses the grid to create contrast between wide and narrow column measures and large and small graphic elements. On an emotional level, the neutral intervals of the grid stand in contrast with the expressive quality of the photos. As with all good design, orchestration is everything.*

R.L.

The Emmett Courant
"The grid represents the basic foundation for the placement of all elements on a page," explains newspaper designer Mario Garcia. For the redesign of the *Emmett Courant* in the Netherlands, Garcia produced a 16-column grid which promotes efficient page makeup and helps give the newspaper a visual identity. The grid interval is a constant in which a pattern can be maintained through changes in text, graphics, and photographs.

The internal spatial relations of the grid can be seen as authoritative markers (like a musical staff) providing a structure for the pace and rhythm of the information.

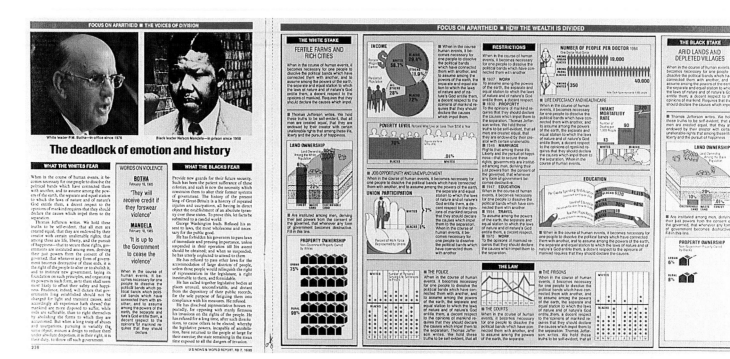

Edwin Taylor:

Finding the appropriate shape of the story

U.S. News & World Report

"There is a natural shape each particular report should take," says newspaper designer Edwin Taylor. "Our job is to search for that shape. The logic of the story dictates that you report it and present it in a certain way" (⊙23). In this gatefold for the prototype of *U.S. News & World Report* done in 1986, Taylor broke down the information into four major segments. Then he developed short, visual packages of information (maps, charts, graphs, photos). But the difficult task was to assemble those pieces in a logical, orderly, and understandable fashion.

The first segment of this Focus on Apartheid is called "The Voices of Division." The conflict and tension are readily apparent in the Botha and Mandela photos, the just-right head, the reversed blocks that head each column, and the box on violence.

The two-page takeout on "How the Wealth is Divided" continues the conflict idea by having "The White Stake" and "The Black Stake" columns flank snippets of important demographic information.

10

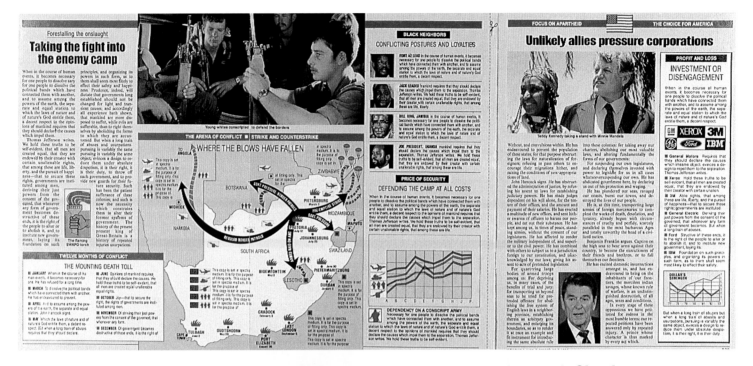

The third segment of the coverage deals with "The Arena of Conflict" and is topped by a photo of white South African soldiers with weapons in hand exhibiting what might be called "calm anxiety." Below the photo is a map with excellent labeling showing the areas of trouble.

Mindful that *U.S. News & World Report* is an American publication, Taylor concludes with a segment that deals with America's role in the South African dilemma.

Structure

The underlying structure of these pages pulls together separate elements, which are then woven into a theme that forms the larger picture.

R.L.

Walter Bernard:

Imagining Time magazine as a newspaper

Cultural constraints

The reality we inhabit is a cultural construct; the shapes and forms we express are constrained by our cultural biases. For instance, in Western culture we "read" a newspaper or a painting from left to right. In the 5th century B.C., Greek lapidary writing was read alternately from left to right and right to left.

R.L.

Time after Time

"In 1980 *Time* magazine was moving back its closing time from Thursday and Friday to Friday and Saturday," says Walter Bernard, publications designer. "The magazine began its press run on Saturday, which continued into Sunday for Monday delivery. It was increasingly processing news stories much like a daily newspaper.

"I wanted to explore what *Time* would look like as a daily broadsheet if it had the capacity to print color and produce the same kind of information graphics and typography we were generating on an increasingly tight schedule."

Above is a design (prepared for a lecture at a newspaper design conference) of *Time* as a broadsheet for Oct. 27, 1980.

USA TODAY, of course, did produce a broadsheet in color with graphics on a daily basis by 1982.

USA Today

This packaged, market-driven newspaper showed publishers that quality reproduction and a lively presentation help sell newspapers. It led the way so that graphics multiplied and eventually migrated to newspapers as traditional as *The New York Times* and *The Wall Street Journal*.

"Visual reporting has to catch your attention," explains Richard Curtis, *USA TODAY*'s managing editor for photography, graphics, and design. "It has to make certain promises; it — coupled with the story you will then read — has to deliver on those promises. Words adequately described Joe Paterno and Jet No. 987 (below). But who would have bothered to stop the race through their daily lives to read and understand?

"Visual reporting is now expected by readers. We've conditioned them to expect it, through newspapers, magazines, television, advertising. Visual reporting helps readers through their daily lives. It organizes information quickly and makes consumption easy, even of the most unappetizing morsels. Plus, it's fun and makes what you put on your plate a little easier to swallow."

Richard Curtis:
Practicing visual reporting

Nigel Holmes:
Exploring symbolic thinking

Connections

The clever use of ancient and modern styles in two and three dimensions in the George Washington logo (right) shows the visual freedom journalists have to express themselves. This playful mix of historic styles requires an understanding of both history and art. In this graphic, Holmes combined two aspects of visual thinking: the naturalistic and the symbolic.

R.L.

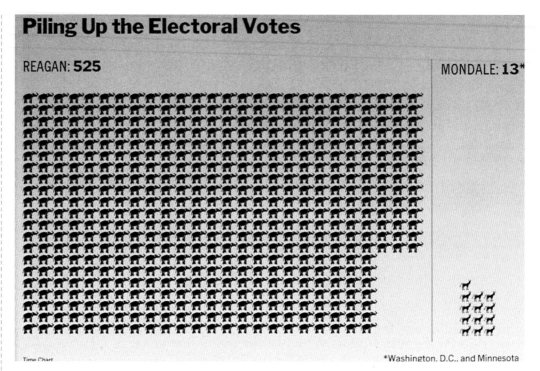

Piling Up the Electoral Votes

REAGAN: **525**

MONDALE: **13***

Time Chart

*Washington. D.C.. and Minnesota

Sending primary signals to readers

Form and content are congruent. The visualization of the Reagan-Mondale election results (above) gives the reader a much quicker "read" of the story than if it had been told only in the text.

Metaphors be with you

Nigel Holmes in his book *Designing Pictorial Symbols* writes that a symbol "attempts to get at the essence of an idea — either by being a literal, miniature drawing, or by being a nonliteral, visual metaphor. A symbol can give an identity to a subject and, by repeated use, can come to equal it."

Robert Lockwood:
Helping readers navigate through the news

The front page as an information graphic

A concern for readers' time has become an essential part of many newspaper redesign efforts. Just because newspapers deliver information doesn't mean readers are informed. We need to deliver the news *and* help readers navigate through it. The prototype (above, left) was the result of explorations for a total graphic approach to the front page for a group of newspapers in Italy (75). Its genesis was a front page I did for *The* (Allentown, Pa.) *Morning Call* in 1979. With a good map and clear signs, readers can choose their pathways and speeds. The extensive use of primary signals directs readers to locations on the map and to a fuller news report inside (114).

Visual language

The newspaper is now seen as a visual language. It considers its audience to be viewers as well as readers. In the best newspaper design content determines the design.

R.L.

15

Section two

The redesign process

A guide to changing newspapers

Planning

The first principle of design

"Design is not a profession – it's an attitude, the attitude of the planner."
Maholy Nagy

Planning is not generally the forte of editors. That might have something to do with the deadline mentality — years of waiting to the last minute before sending copy to the composing room. I once had a feature editor tell me she could not and would not get her section's stories to the printer on time because she dealt with "breaking features." She insisted that her writers wait to the last minute to update their story — every story. She cost the paper thousands of dollars in overtime, but didn't think that was her concern.

In an information society characterized by rapid technological changes, journalists can no longer afford such romanticism. The success of newspapers depends on two things: how well they inform their readers and how well they use information technology to improve their overall performance in a competitive marketplace. This requires anticipation, innovation, and planning.

With each design I try to create a process that involves the total newspaper — from publisher to deliverer. The key is planning. Since the plan determines what you can accomplish, I try to formulate one that encompasses not only the total newspaper, but also the community it serves. In those cases in which the redesign is a radical departure from the past, such as at *The Morning Call* and *The London* (Ontario) *Free Press*, the plan for the redesign of the newspaper included a redesign of the organizations that produced those newspapers (⊙ 42, 94). In any redesign, if you retain the conventional structure of the newsroom, you will inevitably assume the values of the past. To redesign the newspaper you need to redesign the operation. Planning then becomes both an essential prelude and the first principle of design.

Chapter Two of Strunk and White's *The Elements of Style* begins: "Choose a suitable design and hold to it." It goes on to describe the basic principles of composition. Change a few key words, as I've done in the following paragraph, and you have a good definition of planning and newspaper design:

"Perhaps the planning process can best be explained as a series of subconscious conversations which the planner has with himself — the question posed, the factors weighed, and then the recorded conclusion. The more lucid the thinking, the more coherent the powers of idea communication ... the better is the plan."
B. Kenneth Johnstone

A basic structural framework underlies every kind of newspaper design. In part, the journalist will follow this design or deviate from it according to his or her skills and needs and the unexpected events that accompany the act of presenting the news. Newspaper design, to be effective, must closely follow the flow of the news — but not necessarily in the order in which news events occur. This calls for a scheme or procedure. In some cases the best design is no design, as with a late-breaking story, which is simply an outpouring, or with a casual essay, which is a ramble. But in most cases planning must be a deliberate prelude to design. The first principle of design, therefore, is to foresee or determine the shape of what is to come and pursue that shape. The shape the newspaper takes depends on the design approach.

There are basically two approaches to contemporary newspaper design. The first, a mechanical approach, starts with a preconceived idea of what the newspaper should be. Everything fits into a cookie-cutter mold. It's much like the Renaissance architects' insistence that buildings have a predetermined facade, with the addition of pilasters following the hierarchy of the classical orders — the first level, Doric; the second, Ionic; and the third, Corinthian. They placed windows to create a pleasing facade regardless of the function of the rooms inside (⊙ 120).

The second design approach — the one I prefer for newspapers — is a more organic one. Here the design fits more naturally into the environment, much like Frank Lloyd Wright's Fallingwater, in which the shape of the rooms is determined by their function, and the form of the building fits naturally into the environment. There is an underlying structural framework, but the shape is also determined by a more complete view of people and how they live. Through a planning process

Mechanic

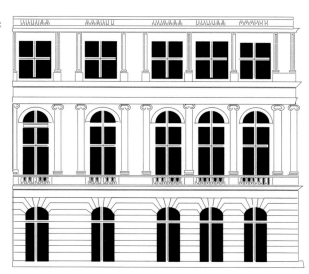

Organic

Reprinted by permission of the Western Pennsylvania Conservancy

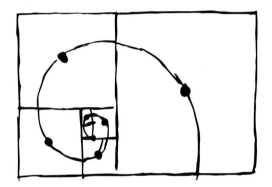

Shaping from within or predetermined from without
The design of the Vitruvius Palazzo in Rome (preceding page) differs in approach from Wright's Fallingwater (above). Le Corbusier (sketches above) followed an organic approach with his design system, the *Modulor*.

that considered his clients' lifestyle, Wright was able to anticipate their needs and create a design solution that was functional and innovative (◉ 121).

What does this have to do with newspaper design? What the examples of redesigns in this book have in common is the design process that led to new looks and directions. The process is organic. It sets up conditions that lead to finding an equilibrium between an underlying structural framework (a grid system) and the process of analyzing the content of the newspaper and the organization that produces it. The results are newspaper designs that are functional and original.

"…let me remind you of a famous passage in which Samuel Taylor Coleridge defined organic form. In a lecture on Shakespeare given in 1818 he made a distinction between what he called mechanic form and organic form. 'Form is mechanic,' he said, 'when on any given material we impress a predetermined form, not necessarily arising out of the properties of the material.' Organic form, on the other hand, is innate; shaping itself from within, as it develops, so that 'the fullness of its development is one and the same with the perfection of its outward form.'"
Jacob Bronowski
Mathematician and author

The front page news budget suggests ...

INTERNATIONAL
☞ Nigeria hikes oil prices
NATIONAL
☞ Unemployment up
☞ Fed easing credit
☞ Mount St. Helens 10 days later
LOCAL
☞ Power & Light Co. is user-friendly
☞ Cuban refugees in limbo
☞ Moth spraying readied
SPORTS
☞ Flyers win
FEATURES
☞ Picasso at MOMA

... the shapes of the layout blocks, which become ...

... information blocks packaged in narrative or ...

At 'Freedom City' ...

. . . waiting fills the days

The grid system

An underlying framework

15 pts.

News events, like thoughts, come mostly in an unstructured form, without clear sequence or order. So design, like writing, must offer some order, or structure, that gives the clarity. The grid is the framework that supports the packaging of the news, but it must do so without constraints or limitations. It must freeze the ice just enough to permit layout editors to do their acrobatics without falling through. In order to organize the design *and* ensure editorial flexibility, I use a two-layered system. The first is a layout grid built on the leading of the newspaper (shown in the drop-in above), which is a more logical unit of measurement than the traditional one of picas and inches. This offers more precision, both in editorial makeup and composing, because all the measurements in the newspaper can be reduced to no more than four. The crucial element of this grid is the constancy of its intervals between lines. If you change the interval and maintain other constants, the change is radical. The grid is passive and mechanical. Because its internal

... explanatory form. Editors can look at every element ...

... and make every element count by using ...

... their total visual vocabulary of ...

... photographs ...

... graphics ...

... and text.

spatial relationships are invariable and not expressive, its structure is not read as a shape but rather as an authoritative marker indicating pace and rhythm in a neutral field free from emotional activity.

The second layer, the information blocks (architectural enclosures), takes its form from the treatment of the news. This grid is organic and active; it changes as the news changes. Because the news determines the shape of the building blocks, it should also control the architecture and look of the page. The logic of each story suggests the shape and size of each information block, which could be presented in narrative or explanatory form (⊙ 10). Some blocks are best done in a narrative approach — story and picture or story and graphic — a linear way of thinking. Others are best suited to a structural approach — breaking the information down into its separate parts and reassembling them into their appropriate shape — a more visual way of thinking. By choosing one approach or the other an editor can let the news assert itself in its most appropriate form.

"... if the printed word promoted mental uniformity," ABCED-mindedness, *"one-point perspective is the forerunner of refined cartography and of the Cartesian system of coordinates, the source of all later scientific systems using graphs. Essentially, the one-point perspective is just that — a graph applied to the eye for the purpose of mechanizing vision, and thus mind."*
Jose Arquelles

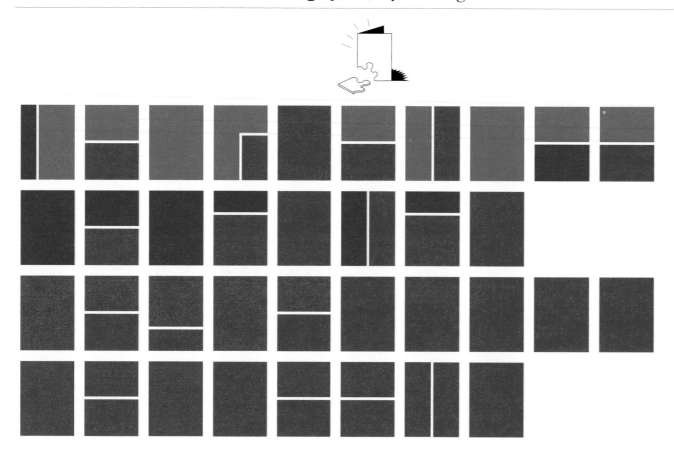

Flat Plan

NATION/WORLD ▬▬
LOCAL ▬▬▬▬
SPORTS ▬▬▬▬
FEATURES ▬▬▬
ADVERTISING ▬▬▬

Design strategy

Design is a powerful strategic tool that newspapers can use to gain a competitive advantage. It can help enhance editorial and advertising shapes and newsroom environments. Any concept of design has to include the organizational structure and managerial climate.
R.L.

Redesign team
Analysis + review = discoveries

The publisher and editor establish the direction the design takes by clarifying the publishing strategy and editorial intent of the newspaper. A design team, representing as many disciplines and departments as are practical, is formed. This democratizes the effort, helps build consensus, and gives as many people as possible a stake in the changes and the future of the newspaper. The design team's role differs from one newspaper to another and depends on the newspaper's resources in terms of both money and talent. But in general, its efforts in the process of analysis and discovery are these:

1. *To gather ideas from editorial, advertising, circulation, and production departments.* The information comes in the form of general design memos from the staff. The design team summarizes the key points made in the staff memos.

2. *To review and analyze content.* This includes a space profile of a typical day's paper, including circulation by edition; by advertising/editorial space per section; by departments (national, international, local, features, business, sports, etc.); by a breakdown of total local news stories

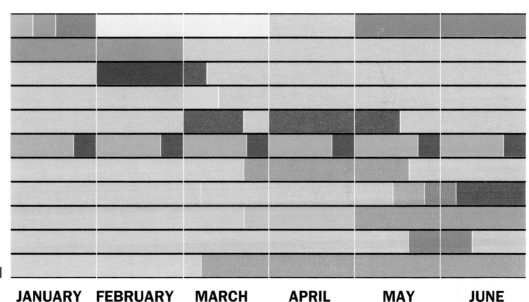

	JANUARY	FEBRUARY	MARCH	APRIL	MAY	JUNE
MARKET RESEARCH						
CONTENT ANALYSIS						
MASTER PROGRAM						
FLAT PLAN						
PROTOTYPES						
CRITICAL REVIEW						
ORDER NEW TYPE, ETC.						
MARKETING PLAN						
STAFF TRAINING						
COMPILE STYLEBOOK						
REORGANIZE NEWSROOM						

used throughout the cycle, including types of stories (government/politics, police/fire, institutional/courts, features, and photographs/graphics) by edition. New editorial approaches to content and presentation are explored and developed.

3. *To review and analyze the operation with an eye toward changes.* The reporters' beats and the strategies of writers and editors are examined in light of a changing world. Beats, news desks, meetings, and writing strategies may have to be changed to meet new goals. New technologies for the newsroom are examined.

4. *To develop a flat plan.* By letting the results of the content review and analysis determine the editorial and advertising shapes on the pages throughout the sections, a logical structure is established from front to back, giving each section a strong beginning, middle, and end, in terms of both advertising and editorial shaping.

The redesign of *The Milwaukee Journal* closely followed the process just described. The design team, led by Sig Gissler, formed subgroups (with whimsical names) to tackle various projects:

☛ The Yardstick Subcommittee analyzed how news spaces were used.
☛ The Nitty Gritty Subcommittee looked at how the paper was assembled.
☛ The Blue Sky Subcommittee explored new ways to serve readers.

Master Plan

The goal is not the flat plan but a master plan that emphasizes the nonstatic nature of the redesign process. The timetable is a visual way to choreograph the process. People can clearly see the various tasks and their relationships to one another. They can also see alternative methods to achieve their goals.
R.L.

☛ The Fly Speck Subcommittee focused on possible gaps in the redesign.

Let's take a closer look at the subcommittees whose task it was to analyze the complex chain of activities in gathering and delivering the news and report their findings to the entire design team.

☛ **The Yardstick Subcommittee** carefully measured the contents of a week's worth of *Journals* and prepared these highlights of its findings: ☞ A graphic summary of the week's ad content and news space — a sort of flat plan in miniature of how the paper was shaped. ☞ Graphs showing which daily staples were consistently positioned and which bounced around. ☞ An analysis of jumps, how they were positioned, and the space they required. (They found that 34 of the 35 stories on Page One on Monday through Saturday jumped. Monday's Page-One stories, their jumps, and sidebar material consumed 40 percent of the news space in the "A" section of the paper.) ☞ An inventory of the use of the "discretionary" space left after the standing features were positioned, the labeled pages were filled, and the cover pages and their jumps were accommodated. ☞ An inventory of photos, graphics, and reader aids. ☞ An inventory of state news content in the main news sections. ☞ Graphs showing the position of editorial and advertising color through the week.

☛ **The Nitty Gritty Subcommittee** was charged with looking at the nuts and bolts of the *Journal's* day-to-day production. They dealt with the following issues: ☞ How does the advertising services department position ads? ☞ They examined the timing and volume of the flow of pages from advertising services, through the newsroom, and on to production. ☞ They documented the newsroom staffing, accounting for each position and the hours needed to accomplish each task.

☛ **The Blue Sky Subcommittee's** mission was to develop ideas for content of the Milwaukee afternoon newspaper of the 1990s. The underlying question was this: If you were to design the perfect newspaper of the 1990s, what would its content be? The task was divided into three phases: (1) The team assembled and reviewed available research information on national and local trends, demographics, and newspaper readership interests, patterns, and habits. (2) They reached a consensus on assumptions about the newspaper of the 1990s and its readers. They also formulated goals based on what they knew about readers' needs. (3) Based on those assumptions and speculation, they brainstormed about content changes (and structural,

---

Memo

THE MILWAUKEE JOURNAL
To: *Desk Heads*
FROM: *Sig Gissler, editor; Steve Hannah, managing editor*
RE: *The New Design*

Print journalism is an entirely visual act of communication — of gathering and presenting information that people want and need to know to lead effective lives.

The redesign offers exciting journalistic opportunities. We're counting on you, as newsroom leaders, to explain the redesign in staff briefings, to stimulate discussion, and to help generate enthusiasm for improved ways to communicate with our readers.

Here is some help with questions that might come up …

Why are we redesigning the paper?

It has been increasingly clear to us that in order to maintain and build readership in the '90s we have to have a clear focus on our readers' needs. Basically, we want to serve them, just as we always have. But today's readers

packaging, and delivery changes where appropriate) that would enhance the readership and quality of the newspaper. At this point there was no attempt to assemble a model or grand plan. The objective was to imagine the possible based on how readers were likely to use the newspaper. From this process several themes emerged:

☞ **The macro/micro approach.** Give readers both the big picture and the narrow focus, the quick summary and in-depth coverage; both the global news and the explanatory package showing how this event affects a household; both the who-what-where-when-why and what-you-can-do-about-it; both indexing and substantial information worth indexing.

☞ **Management for maximum creativity.** The content of the newspaper can improve if the newsroom is managed at all levels in ways that promote creativity. Encourage people to take more risks, and do away with preconceptions about stories. Encourage and enhance communication with people about assignments, content, and packaging information.

☞ **The graying of the readers.** Babyboomers are getting older. Fifty percent more readers will be in the 35–54 age group over the next decade. At the same time, we need to be concerned about attracting younger audiences before our older readers die.

☞ **The value of indexing.** If we're going to make the newspaper more useful to readers of the 1990s, one key is going to be indexing what's in the paper, what's in other media, what's in future papers, what was in past papers, what's going on in town tonight, where the bargains are, and everything else that helps direct readers to the information they need to make choices.

☞ **The global village.** An understanding of the world — not just news events — is going to be increasingly important in the lives of readers because of environmental concerns, information technology, global trade, and economic competition.

☞ **The growing minority population.** The greatest single opportunity for greater readership and circulation rests with the various minority groups in Milwaukee who are not reading the newspaper.

☞ **Our bread and butter: news.** Covering good old-fashioned news is still going to be a key to our quality in the 1990s. Above all else, the redesign of the newspaper needs to emphasize the core mission: to seek

are different from readers of yesteryear. Readers today are more time-stressed than ever. Many read us thoroughly. Others say they often don't have time. We want all readers to know that they DO have time to read a paper that is sensitive to their busy schedules: one that will continue to offer them the depth they expect and demand from *The Journal* but provide them with easier pathways into the wealth of information presented there each day. Reader service — that is at the heart and soul of the redesign.

How is this redesign going to change the life of the reporter?

Frankly, good stories will get better display. We will have fewer tops on Page One most days, giving the stories that make it better display. The windows on the front page will provide a strong reference point: inside Part A, in Sports, in Business, in Features. We're going to do a better job than ever of bringing readers inside the paper each day. We're going to intensify readership.

Yes, some stories may be capsulized on Page One but with a strong reference to better display for the narrative, graphics, and pictures inside.

More teamwork with photographers and artists often will produce packages

out truth amid increasing confusion, to serve readers as a watchdog for public and private institutions, and to investigate wrongdoing.

The design committee used the findings of the subcommittees to create a master plan. This became the model for the prototype. The prototype gave us a blueprint for the structure and look of the newspaper. This in turn became the guideline that led to the reorganization of the newsroom.

☞ **The Fly Speck Subcommittee** reviewed the process at each stage to see if we missed anything.

One result of the design team's efforts was a reorganization of the news operations: photo and art departments were integrated into the news department, staff and space were added, new technology was introduced, and changes were made in typography, layout, and packaging.

The goal of this reorganization was to improve the link between staff and the resulting product. On one level the results provided better coordination among reporters, photographers, and artists. We were able to get people to embrace the same goals and speak the same language. On another level it resulted in better coordination between news, production, and systems departments to benefit the newspaper as a whole and not just individual departments. As the process advanced, Editor Sig Gissler was careful to tell folks at the paper why we were doing what we were doing and why it was important.

During the redesign process it's important to look for opportunities to improve existing interdepartmental ties or find new ones. I generally try to coordinate activities between different departments to benefit the newspaper as a whole, not just the individual departments. At the end a master program for change in the organization emerges. The program becomes a flexible guide to renewing the organization rather than fixed rules handed down from above. A timetable is created to put the program into effect.

---

that will free narrative of statistical details.

What about copy editors?

The role of the editor will become increasingly important in the '90s. Right from the start, there will be those summary decks to write. As we deliberately choose to use many visual points of entry into a story, we expect that the copy will determine the best way to tell a story. Is a narrative enough? Should it be a narrative and a graphic? What should be graphic? What about pictures? These are questions that copy editors will increasingly become involved in working with reporters and members of the graphics team. We think layout opportunities will increase for copy editors, too.

Are we going to be formula-driven?

Actually, we will be less formula-driven than we are now. Right now, if you check a series of our front pages, we generally run six stories, day after day.

With the redesign, the shape of the page will be more driven by the shape of the news. Even the size and shape of the windows will be determined by the news. We may have three stories out front; we may have four; we may have five. On a rare news day — or on a day with a fabulous writing job or stunning photography — we may go with one or two.

The prototype

This 1990 prototype of the redesign of *The Milwaukee Journal* was the result of an extensive process of review and analysis of the total newspaper — the product, the operation, and the community. The results of that effort determined the editorial and advertising restructuring under the direction of editor Sig Gissler.

As John Gardner observed, "All human systems require continuous renewal. They rigidify. They get stiff in the joints. They forget what they cared about. The forces against it are nostalgia and the enormous appeal of having things the way they have always been … but we've got to move on."

Reader reaction

Eighty-seven percent thought the paper was "keeping up with the times." Seventy percent said it was "better organized and easier to read." Sixty-five percent said it was "more lively." Sixty percent said it was a "better use of reading time." Fifty-six percent thought "there were more stories." Fifty-four percent said the "quality of the stories improved."

The prototype
A search for vitality

At the prototype stage I work closely with the editor and the design team to determine what shape the redesign should take. Then we work up possibilities based on our discussions. The course chosen is based on the special needs of the reader and is tailored to the paper's editorial and marketing goals. A style is then developed, in the form of a prototype, that is applied to the total paper. The result is a paper that's cohesive, with all parts relating to the whole. Achieving this requires building a logical structure, or architecture, for both advertising and editorial layout. The objective is to help the reader find and understand the content easily.

After working out a "style" for the front page, where we want to create the tone and character of the newspaper, I continue to develop design ideas throughout the paper. At each stage of the redesign I offer options. For example, I offer at least three front-page possibilities, each suggesting a different approach in terms of layout, typefaces, etc. With these objectives in mind, I try to make the design original and indigenous to the newspaper's location.

An original design
There are two forms of originality. The scope of the changes desired will determine which form is appropriate for the newspaper. The first form, which involves the inventing of new rules, leads to radical change, much like the 1979 redesign of *The Morning Call* in Allentown, Pa., and the 1989 redesign of *The London* (Ontario) *Free Press* (⊙ 42, 94). The second form doesn't concern itself so much with changing rules as it does with discovering new ways of operating within established rules. This results in more conservative designs such as the New York *Daily News* and *The Milwaukee Journal* (⊙ 68).

An indigenous design
Because it must work for the reader in a particular community, the design should capture the special spirit of the circulation area. I like to practice what I call indigenous designing because I believe a newspaper, like a building, should fit naturally into its community. Consequently, I try to tailor each design to fit the newspaper's particular readership and specific locale (⊙ 87, 133).

Inventing new rules and working within established ones

The goal of the 1989 redesign of *The London* **(Ontario)** *Free Press* **was to create a totally different approach to producing newspapers. The project involved reshaping the newspaper and the news operation. The 1985 redesign of the New York** *Daily News,* **on the other hand, was aimed at enhancing the newspaper in content and form while retaining a traditional approach to news gathering and presentation.**

I do this by talking with people in the newspaper, reviewing readership studies, and studying the history of the area and the newspaper's relationship to it. The design committee's work helps here. I spend time in the city, eat in its restaurants, study its architecture, and look for those details that distinguish one community from another.

Each design, then, operates in the context of its particular culture.

Indigenous designs *are attentive to the stake readers have in the newspaper, appropriate to the community served, and organized in a way that presents information by stressing content over design inventiveness.* **R.L.**

31

10 redesign steps

Putting it all together

1.

Planning

A prelude to design

The publisher and editor set a clear course by clarifying the publishing strategy and editorial direction of the paper. They identify opportunities for enhancement of the total newspaper including editorial, circulation, production, and advertising departments. They agree on a design approach and implementation date (⊙ 19).

2.

Redesign committees

Giving people a say in their future

A design committee, made up of managers and staff from editorial, advertising, circulation, and production departments, is formed. Sometimes a separate committee is assigned to study publishing strategy while another performs the more tactical work of studying the paper. The committees receive data and ideas from people in all departments (⊙ 24).

Illustrations by Nigel Holmes

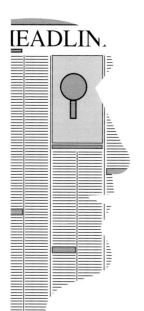

3.

Taking inventory
Making discoveries

An inventory is made of each part of the newspaper: the news report, the readers, the market, the community, new technology (◉ 24).

4.

Timetable
The dating game

A realistic timetable is established, starting with the implementation date and then working back (◉ 25).

5.

Critical review *Examining the present with an eye toward the future*

Senior editors examine ideas developed by design groups and evaluate each element that makes up the daily report — in effect, redefining the purpose and direction of each part of the paper (◉ 25).

44. Documentation/instructions
45. Dummies/scale
46. Editions
47. Editorial intentions
48. Education
49. Ergonomics
50. Ethics
51. Excitement vs. dullness; energy, quiet
52. Fixed/fluid information
53. Flat plan
54. Flow, sequence, placement
55. Form/function
56. Format
57. Formula vs. freedom, how much flexibility
58. Future: tomorrow's newspaper, new, innovation
59. Geography
60. Geometry
61. Goals, objectives, planning
62. Grids
63. Harmony
64. Headlines: type, styles, formats
65. Hierarchy
66. Icons
67. Ideas
68. Implementation: schedule, steps
69. Indexing
70. Information blocks
71. Information: fixed, fluid
72. Inside pages
73. Integration of words and images
74. Italics
75. Journalists
76. Jumps
77. Labels
78. Layout
79. Legibility
80. Liaison, management, design committee
81. Logos
82. Logotype
83. Makeup: modular, horizontal, vertical
84. Management
85. Maps: locator, metaphorical, mental, topographical, projections, weather, networks, and routes

33

6.

The flat plan
Where ideas assume their logical shape

The flat plan, a model of carefully planned editorial and advertising spaces, allows the editors to pay special attention to the pace and rhythm of the presentation and the quality of the shapes (24).

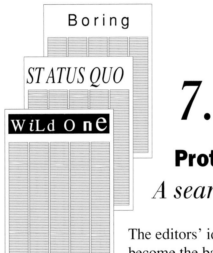

7.

Prototypes
A search for vitality

The editors' ideas and the design group's findings become the basis for prototypes. The tone and character of the paper are worked out on the front page with the designer showing options for consideration by management and staff (30).

8.

Technical considerations
Developing new layout grids, ordering typefaces, ordering and formatting new systems

After the prototype is approved, new grid sheets and typefaces must be ordered and preparations made to reformat codes. Advertising and promotion strategies should be set, and newsroom and production changes needed to support the new design should be put in place (22, 130).

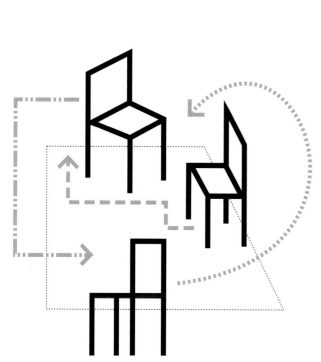

9.

Newsroom reorganization

Freeing people from the inhibiting world of hierarchy

Newspaper design is as much about moving chairs around in the newsroom as moving type around on a page. If you simply superimpose a new design on old structures, you'll get the old design in new clothing. If successful, the redesign process helps to coordinate departments to benefit the newspaper as a whole. It gives clarity to editorial ambitions. The purpose of training and newsroom reorganization — which go hand in hand — is to get people to speak the same language and embrace complementary goals (⊙ 118).

10.

Implementation

Making the design come alive

Readers tend to readily accept changes that are substantive and not merely cosmetic. A gradual implementation is easier on both staff and readers, especially when the changes are innovative. In all cases, readers and staff should be advised of the changes before they take place (⊙ 26).

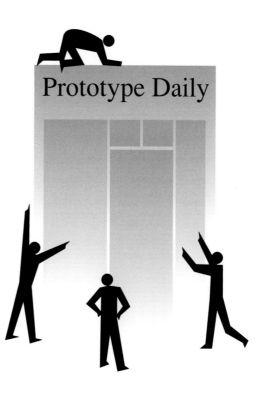

Prototype Daily

Section three

Case studies

The responsibility of form

Form and content

Reshaping the newspaper

In the TV age we all suffer from Hype-nosis.

Traditionally newspaper design dealt solely with the shape and form of the product. This often produced newspapers that were beautiful but that tended to remove energy from style.

Newspaper design today is still seen mostly as content shaped into form. It can also be viewed as energy and its dynamic organization — a view of news design that involves the total newspaper. This view appreciates the nonstatic nature of news and stresses the connection between people and the organization (• 122).

The responsibility of form, in this concept, is to liberate words and images from the inhibiting world of objects and people from the inhibiting world of outdated structures. In other words, we must create more flexible forms for both the organization and the newspaper itself (• 118). Any concept of newspaper design today has to include the development of more flexible management systems and recognize that staff quality is the keystone of a good newspaper.

The seven case studies in this section were written by editors from some of the newspapers I've redesigned in the last decade. They all make the case for design as a process, as an attitude about information, as an organizational structure — but not as decoration or typographical flights of fancy.

In some of the projects we tried to find ways to broaden and deepen our definition of the news. A few projects were attempts at redefining what a newspaper is. What all the projects have in common is a desire to meet readers' needs.

Redesign
Most questions worth asking have no absolute answers, and the themes worth examining have no definite endings. A redesign is not a final destination; it's a way of involving many people over a period of time. This involvement creates chains of experience that help build a new culture within the organization.
R.L.

Case study one

The Morning Call

THE MORNING CALL

City/State
Allentown, Pa.
Circulation:
Daily (a.m.): 118,577
Sunday: 155,118
Date of
Implementation:
February 1978
Executive Editor:
Edward Miller
Managing Editor:
Jerry Bellune
Design:
Robert Lockwood
Art Director:
Jeff Lindenmuth
Typography:
Body Type:
Crown
Headline Typeface:
Univers
Section Flags and
Column Logo Typefaces:
Stymie Bold, Helvetica
Bold, and Helvetica
Extra Bold

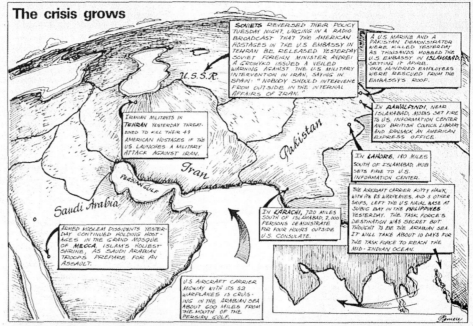

THE IRANIAN CRISIS: DAY 19

Americans rescued as embassy burns in Pakistan

▶Marine slain. A12

Militants vow to kill hostages if U.S. attacks

INSIDE

Islam's new fervor
The world's 800 million Moslems entered Islam's 15th century yesterday with a new fervor fueled by oil dollars and manifested in Iran's radical fundamentalism.
A2

A crowd estimated at up to two million people converged on the occupied U.S. Embassy in Iran, where militants threatened to kill their 49 American hostages if the United States attempts to use military force against Iran.
A2

Soviets change broadcast tune
A Soviet-controlled radio station that broadcasts to Iran now is urging the release of American hostages at the U.S. Embassy in Tehran, making "180-degree shift" from its previous stance.
A2

U.S. has several military options

By FRED S. HOFFMAN
Of The Associated Press

WASHINGTON — A buildup of U.S. Navy carrier striking power in the Indian Ocean-Arabian Sea area will enable President Carter to order retaliatory strikes against Iran if American hostages are killed.

The Carter administration is carefully avoiding any public commitment to an option or set of options, but the threat of possible retribution is considered the most plausible course of action for the United States if the Americans held in the U.S. embassy in Tehran are slain.

Military planners discount the practicality of any rescue mission into Tehran, saying such an effort most likely would lead to the instant deaths of the Americans, who have been prisoners of Iranian students for 17 days.

Please See OPTIONS Page A13▶

THE MORNING CALL

Ready for prime time

Inventing new ways to present the news

by Edward D. Miller

The internal pressures of the news determine the design.

The Morning Call, in Allentown, Pa., was fertile ground for change in the 1970s. Profitable and still locally owned, it had an editor yearning to create something significant and a creative staff equal to the challenge. We can skip the psychoanalysis and admit the obvious: Newspapers change, strive, and succeed because ego-driven people harness a vision to advantageous circumstances. For a few years in the late 1970s and early 1980s, such a vision met these circumstances in Allentown.

To understand the look of the paper, you first have to understand the environment in which it was produced. A grandson of the paper's founding patriarch was the editor and soon-to-be publisher. Not surprisingly, the staff was split between the Radicals, usually but not always the younger and newer staffers who wanted to experiment and change, and the Resisters, often the old hands for whom the old ways were a successful standard to be defended. Most revolutions are waged between similarly armed camps.

The Old Guard had produced a fine paper for its time. Its style had an orderly, comfortable feeling that convinced readers the editors had sorted through a messy pile of the day's news and tidied up the bits and pieces for presentation in print. *The Call* came into the home as a trusted and well-mannered acquaintance dressed in a three-piece suit and speaking in well-mannered tones, seldom shouting or disrupting, a gentleman of conservative style and taste.

But something was missing. The paper's stuffy personality lacked the wit and whimsy of the poet. Only occasionally did it sing, and then only familiar folk tunes, never rock 'n' roll. It was dull and predictable. When researcher Joe Belden first saw the paper in 1975, he told me, "Ed, you have a handsome newspaper … for the 1940s." He was being polite.

Part of the problem was generational. The editors were disciplined, competent men, but sons of another era. (Most women on the editorial staff were still confined to the "women's section.") For the editors, television was an amusing novelty, a commercial competitor to be sure, but not a factor to be contended with in news coverage. They knew their community intimately — every street, every over-the-hill politician,

Edward D. Miller is an associate of the Poynter Institute for Media Studies in St. Petersburg, Fla.

A graduate of Williams College, Miller began his career on the *International Edition* of the *New York Herald Tribune* in Paris. From 1969 to 1981 he was editor of *The Morning Call* in Allentown, Pa. He was named publisher of the paper in 1979.

He is a former director and officer of the Associated Press Managing Editors Association (APME) and a former director of the American Society of Newspaper Editors (ASNE).

He was cofounder of the Society of Newspaper Design (SND) and the First Amendment Coalition of Pennsylvania.

THE MORNING CALL

Before

Readers need to search for signs of life beneath the surface.

Design logic

The logic of a story dictates how you report and present it. With labels and other devices such as logos, summaries, and chapter heads within the story, we enable readers to move through the information.
R.L.

What we learned

1. *The product reflects the organization.*

Here's an axiom you can wager on: A rigid, authoritarian organization pursuing narrowly defined objectives will be populated by people of similar conviction. Furthermore, the product of their labors will be predictably rigid and unimaginatively conventional.

The correlation between the nature of the staff and the product it produces is untested in the literature of psychology, but the evidence is plentiful. People who are by nature

every ancient sports hero. They never missed a thing in obits. Yet these same editors were strangely isolated from readers; they seldom ventured out to report, give speeches, meet the public, wrestle with the readers. Theirs was an insider's routine.

Nuts-and-bolts meeting coverage was the paper's meat and potatoes. Readers were fed a "paper of record," a comprehensive bulletin board of official spokesmen and meeting reports, a thorough digest of the region's organized activities. The paper had the appearance of thoroughness, but along the way it missed most of the major trend stories of its day. Investigative reporting was rare. It was not considered polite to be aggressive, and these were polite men, town criers rather than pamphleteers.

It may be unfair to fault one generation for not seeing the needs of the next, particularly when there was no pressing reason to change. The publisher was satisfied; his newspaper was competent, respected in the industry, and acceptable to the town's opinion makers. His sacred cows found green pastures in the pages of his newspaper, which in turn was profitable and honored in its own land. Why change?

THE MORNING CALL

The shape of the news

The design of The Call *began with the conviction that the news should determine the shape of the story and the look of the page. In addition, we attempted to make the information more accessible to readers.*
R.L.

By the 1970s, change was no longer a choice. It was a fact. By then, America was aflame with the fires of Vietnam, the youth revolution, feminism, civil rights, gay rights, and the environment. Issues that had been pent up, unorganized, unexploited, and underplayed in the nation's media were now exploding on the streets and in the news.

People's perceptions were changing, too. It was not an illusion; life really was more complex. Even when we strip away the veil of nostalgia tinting our view of the past, we can look across the divide of the 1960s and see a simpler time. For women, blacks, the poor, the handicapped, and all those denied access and influence, "simpler" was not necessarily better. But for the rest of us, the past was less complicated, buttressed by relationships between races, between men and women, between young and old that had been "understood" for generations. As these "understandings" changed, our perception began to correlate with fact, forcing newspapers to look at the world differently. To take that different look, *The Morning Call* had to transform both the organization and the mythology that supported it. Initially there was no "plan," only a belief that change was needed. Progress lurched. An idea would emerge, a few people with the power to push it forward would push. Sometimes the idea moved, but just as often it got stuck in the muck of tradition or was derailed by people with a

innovative, experimental, and attuned to the needs and wants of the marketplace will produce products that reflect those characteristics. It's no coincidence that the bean-curd-and-sprouts crowd drawn to Silicon Valley demanded unusual corporate environments and also produced countless innovations. In contrast are the dogmatic people who assume they know what the market needs and will, by God, give it to them, whether consumers want it or not. They invariably produce unimaginative products that are vulnerable to shifting market conditions. Too many editors fit the second description.

THE MORNING CALL

2. *People can accomplish more than their job descriptions would predict. Labels confine, constrain.*

Everyone likes to believe his or her own life and work is special, that his or her presence on the planet makes a difference. Yet so often we create and manage organizations as if they were machines. People are categorized, compartmentalized, segregated by their skills and given tasks instead of goals, duties instead of challenges.

Rationalizations about deadlines, stockholders, and profits encourage people to value efficiency over effectiveness. Over time, however, people deprived of a creative atmosphere adjust by either suffocating their creative urges or leaving the organization to find more refreshing air elsewhere.

We tried to create an atmosphere in which individuals could express their vision in terms beyond service to the organization. The organization was important, for collectively we could do more than any of us could do individually, but we tried to nurture the individual spark by thinking of the organization as a room full of freelancers coming together on projects of mutual interest.

We seldom succeeded. It was a difficult task with few models to study, but there were enough triumphs to convince us that the human spirit, working in an organization that nurtures instead of dictates, can indeed liberate imagination and energy to create works of penetrating vision.

stake in the status quo. The laws of inertia were as instructive as any journalism text: "A body at rest tends to stay at rest; a body in motion tends to stay in motion." The trick was to get the bodies in motion and keep them moving. Direction was less important than momentum.

A change in attitude was crucial. If the newspaper were to help readers comprehend a changing world, the newspaper itself would have to learn how to accommodate change, not as a once-and-done housecleaning, but as a way of life. Most organizations resist change. In newspapers, human tendencies to establish hierarchies and fix routines often conspire with traditional union work rules to perpetuate a rigid caste system. Reporters write but aren't supposed to draw, photograph, or make judgments on the news. Photographers take pictures but seldom write and never design the front page. A sense of craftsmanship has withered under this strict segregation of skills and a companion drive to automate. We have lost touch with our heritage of craftsmen who would master many skills along an intricate path toward the making of a Kentucky rifle or a Chippendale chair or a silver bowl. At *The Call* we tried to restore some of that vision and overall responsibility by coaxing reporters to explore an idea in words and pictures and then help design the final page. The results were invariably more exciting and successful. A reporter told me one time you can always tell how much of himself a writer puts into a story by the fingerprints on his copy. These early design efforts had people's fingerprints all over them.

We always tried to keep in mind that the objective of these changed attitudes and practices was to add life and energy to a dull newspaper. News itself is not dull; editors bleach it colorless. Attend a news meeting at any newspaper and feel the excitement, humor, tragedy, irony, and outrage of human events. Discussions are animated as editors summarize for one another the plot of yet another human tale. But something is lost on the way to the newsprint. The bright emotions fade as we scrub and polish the news and fit it into conventions.

Writers trot out a tired formula, like the tradition-sanctified "inverted pyramid," and proceed to work the equation instead of tell the tale. Layout editors begin page assembly by ranking the news — "this is a lead, this is a sublead, this goes in the roundup" — a hierarchy of geopolitical importance that would please any social studies teacher. Occasionally a "human interest" piece breaks into the hierarchy for comic relief, but our

We see things as we do because of what we expect them to look like.

THE MORNING CALL

Subtle indexing

Readers should be led to new information that is relevant to their needs without their knowing exactly what they wanted beforehand, thus providing opportunities for more subtle forms of browsing.

R.L.

calling it "human interest" exposes the rest of the page to be of interest to someone other than humans.

Many editors seem to have a vertical, one-two-three mind. Maybe it's the influence of sports, with its winners and losers, standings, and computer ratings. Eventually everything in a paper is ranked, a lead story to a filler, front page to inside, A to G section. It's as if the news had to pass through a gate leading to a narrow tunnel. Only one story at a time fits through. On the way through the gate, stories march in lockstep and single file. Sometimes, when sidebars are used, a "column-of-twos" is permitted, but soon it's back to single file, with the least being last. But news is far more complex than that. Russian efforts to open up local elections to dissident candidates cannot be isolated from American agricultural policy. A Japanese decision to market HDTV is a "lead story" in the Sears board room. Editors know this, but they are often too lazy to make the connections. They expect the AP or The New York Times News Service to make sense of the pieces by completing the puzzle for them in "analysis" pieces. They don't see that "analysis" is an integral function of a news story, which to most readers is no longer "news" anyway.

3. *"Information dictates the design."*

Editors are fond of citing chapter and verse from journalism scripture that says that the importance of the news story will determine its play in the paper. When you accuse editors of stuffing news into preconceived formats, their indignation wells up as they defend their challenged honor.

The truth is they design by pigeonhole most of the time. That's what a lead story is: the biggest, most prominent pigeonhole in the paper. Ask an editor what he does on a day when there is no "lead story." He won't understand the question: "There *has* to be a lead story."

THE MORNING CALL

The front page as an information graphic

With print all information is visual. A page of text or a page of photographs, each has the impact of an information graphic. The way you place the words, graphics, and photographs on the page must confirm and support that day's news (⊙ 15).

R.L.

No, there doesn't, any more than there *has* to be a collection of five to seven smaller stories to put into the news summary, or three items to put in the promotion boxes across the top. These are conventions of layout, pigeonholes waiting for pigeons. They have nothing to do with "design."

The nature and characteristics of the information will tell you how to design. Look at the phone book. Its name-rank-and-phone number design is predicated by the nature of the information itself. Imagine baseball standings in a narrative format, or death notices not beginning with the person's name.

To do the puzzle ourselves requires abandoning the linear, the vertical, the straight-line march through the tunnel. It means thinking laterally, seeing the connections between the unconnected. That's what we tried to do with front pages in Allentown. Each day was a blank canvas. We didn't need a "lead story"; we could make our own. If the news came through as a series of seemingly unconnected visual images, we connected them, never pretending that this pattern was "news," only that we recognized a pattern and chose to display the pieces in that particular framework. We gave readers credit for good sense. We believed readers would understand that some days there is no "big story," that a screaming headline on a wimpy story sends the wrong message about both the story and your devices for communicating news, that a day with a created front page, such as an unusual handling of post-election material, would work only if the device made sense to the reader. In other words, the nature of the news and information had to dictate the design. At most papers the process is backwards; the design or format of the front page is essentially predetermined, a dirty little secret editors don't like to admit. But for proof just look at most newspapers. Promo boxes go over the top every

THE MORNING CALL

day, whether or not there's anything inside worth promoting. A digest covers the bottom of the page, insensitive to the nuances and subtleties of the content. The page-one columnist, dull or delightful, is always run down the left side. The above-the-fold photograph will be in color, even if there is a better black-and-white available, for how else can expensive color equipment be justified? French paté makers would applaud how we stuff our goose with news. But the result is seldom digestible. To avoid the dull and actually deal with the news in a way that made more sense to the reader, we tried to create and sustain a climate of experimentation, daring, and inventiveness, not for their own sake, but in the interest of capturing the readers' attention and fancy. Somewhere in that process, we believed, communication would result in perception and understanding.

As we experimented, we learned how to expand our thinking. We believed, for example, that the "newspaper" of the future would be quite different, that advances in technology would permit multiple means of delivering information, especially via computers and phone links directly to the readers. A decade ago we could see the Buck Rogers era coming,

Extending the logic of these obvious examples to front-page news is the conceptual leap we tried to make in Allentown. An example is news the day after an election. One editor put it simply: "People want to know *what* happened, *why* it happened, and *what's next*." The page was designed around those three questions. A single essay would not have worked as well. A "lead" story would have diverted too much attention to one factor or diluted the essentially tripartite nature of the news that day. Conventional headlines would get in the way; only the questions themselves would do for headings. Once again, "the information dictates the design."

49

THE MORNING CALL

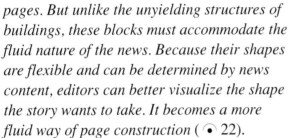

Information blocks as flexible templates

Information blocks are the building blocks (architecture) of these pages. But unlike the unyielding structures of buildings, these blocks must accommodate the fluid nature of the news. Because their shapes are flexible and can be determined by news content, editors can better visualize the shape the story wants to take. It becomes a more fluid way of page construction (⚲ 22).
R.L.

4. *Readers will tolerate anything that works.*

So often editors of other papers would ask, "How did your readers react to your radical designs?" The answer was simple. They didn't. They didn't see anything "radical" in packaging that tried to make sense of a confused world, in presentations of information that they did not see on television last night. William Zinsser says we are not in the "news" business at all, that we are in the "meaning" business. Our designs tried to convey meaning as opposed to collections of news bites. I think readers can sense the difference and respond accordingly.

yet no one knew exactly how to prepare for it. It seemed to us that only two factors were central to coping with a different future — a flexible staff capable of adaptation to new technology and the information itself. To develop the staff for the future, we tried all sorts of things. Editors went to art school to better understand visual presentation of information. (Recruiting for that class was easy; one of the last sessions was sketching nudes.) A reporter was sent to medical school for a year to help us keep pace with a continuing major story. A professor of management was hired to help us understand organizational behavior. A newspaper-in-education program was expanded to include the production of several local high school papers, a step we hoped would provide talented staffers in the next generation.

To develop an information base, we spent hundreds of thousands of dollars computerizing the library. We were convinced that we had to begin learning how to use the sophisticated tools of database management and that the library would be the center of that process, not merely a service appendage to the newsroom.

THE MORNING CALL

A strategy started to take shape; it held that information, not just the delivery of inked newsprint, was central to our survival and profitability. All the training, all the investment in people and equipment had one focus: how could we make the newspaper *essential* to readers? Not just convenient, not simply entertaining, but essential. We even concocted an ersatz Latin motto: "*Nobis Propositum Necessarium Est:* Our Purpose Is To Be Essential."

Did any of this work? Was the revolution a success? That depends on how you keep score. Readers in Allentown had come to accept radical design as part of *The Morning Call*, so the lack of routine became routine. After we changed specific parts of the paper — for example, converting a dull Saturday a.m. broadsheet to a lively, younger-reader-oriented tabloid — we watched circulation figures go up. Similarly, changes in the Sunday package were followed by observable gains in readers.

5. *To redesign a paper, first redesign the publisher.*

To properly redesign a paper, you have to change the people. Because the publisher is the ultimate designer of a newspaper (he determines the size of the staff and budget), he needs to be redesigned first. He also sets the tone and spirit of the news operation. A conventional, authoritarian, chain-of-command-loving chief of state will assemble an organization that reflects his style and personality. In turn, the paper will reflect that kind of organization.

THE MORNING CALL

But be cautious here. It's a dangerous cause-and-effect connection to say that design features alone produced higher circulation. We firmly believed we were on the right track to attract and retain readers: our household penetration figures were among the highest in our circulation class at that time. The innovative and fresh approach to the news certainly enhanced that relationship with readers, but that's a conclusion that has to be taken on faith, for it's difficult to prove the connection.

Did any of this last? Robert and I left *The Call* in 1981, after which it came under new management. It is still a good newspaper — solid, complete, conventional. But it is not on the leading edge of creative design or management innovation. It is now in a chain (Times-Mirror) and subject to all the advantages and limitations of group ownership.

Was there any lasting impact? That's hard to gauge. We do know that numerous newspapers interested in developing a more dynamic look and approach to readers were aware of the innovations in Allentown. Founding editors of *USA TODAY*, for example, took comfort in the Allentown experience that readers would tolerate a wider range of graphic presentations than editors had previously suspected. Other newspapers learned the same lesson.

Robert and I had a hand in the founding of the Society of Newspaper Design, and through that organization spread the word that good design is good business.

Can the "golden years" of Allentown ever be duplicated somewhere else? Certainly, but it will require publishers, editors, artists, and other journalists who understand the link between the way an organization manages itself and the product it puts on the street. Creative design is possible only in a creatively designed organization. That can happen anywhere if people want it to.

Case study two

The Philadelphia Bulletin

The Bulletin

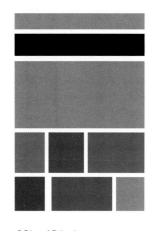

City/State
Philadelphia, Pa.
Circulation:
Daily (a.m.): 434,000
Sunday: 505,000
Date of
Implementation:
September 1980
Publisher:
N. S. ("Buddy") Hayden
Editor:
Craig Ammerman
Design:
Robert Lockwood
Art Director:
Rudy DeFelice
Typography:
Body Type:
Century Schoolbook
Headline Typeface:
Helvetica
Section Flags and
Column Logo
Typefaces:
Helvetica Extra Bold

Congratulations, Pete!

The Bulletin

Tuesday, August 11, 1981   LB

Dedicated to Serving Greater Philadelphia and South Jersey

★4★

25¢

Rose, with Stan Musial at his side, acknowledges the fans' cheers after breaking "The Man's" record.

Bulletin Photo by Salvatore DiMarco Jr.

He's a hit

60,000 fans at Vet go wild over magic 3,631 milestone

By CLAIRE SMITH
Of The Bulletin Staff

She stood in the aisle, her hand-painted "Welcome back, Phillies — Good luck, Pete" sign resting at her feet. All around her, thousands of people were standing and cheering, caught up in the magic of the moment.

But for Joann Dermigny, it was a time just to savor.

"This is just the greatest thing ever," she said quietly, as she looked around Veterans Stadium last night. "I just love Pete Rose."

A lot of people loved Pete Rose last night because the Phillies' first baseman did what Joann and approximately 60,000 other baseball fans had been hoping for. The future Hall of Famer swung at the second pitch from Cardinals reliever Mark Littell in the eighth inning and nubbed a single into left field, giving him 3,631 career hits, a National League record.

On a night when fans and players were saying a tentative hello to each other after a wrenching 50-day strike by the major-leaguers, Rose seized the moment and provided a tonic for the game.

"It takes a Pete Rose to do something like this," Joann Dermigny said as she looked around the Vet at the cheering hordes. "After tonight and after the (1980) World Series, well, it's just the most exciting thing I've ever seen. It's just the greatest."

Rose didn't have to break the record held by Stan Musial for 18 years to impress the 20-year-old resident of Brookhaven, Pa., because, numbers aside, Joann always will remember him for something he once did off the playing field.

"Last March, I wrote a letter to Pete and told him about my brother Mike, who's 11," she explained. "I told him that Mike was going to have open-heart surgery and that he's a big fan of his."

She said she didn't know what to expect, but what she and her brother got back was more than she had hoped for.

"He sent Mike an autographed picture, plus some bumper stickers and a picture of the Phillie Phanatic," she said. "Mike was very excited. And now he's a bigger Pete Rose fan than ever."

Down on the field, Rose approached the plate again

Please see **BIG NIGHT** Page A7

INSIDE

√ Record-breaking hit was a typical effort. By Gerry Fraley. Page D1

√ Pete Rose was an island of cool in an ocean of excitement. Mark Whicker's column. Page D1

√ By numbers alone, Rose has a place in baseball history. By Joe Lunardi. Page D3.

√ Stan Musial was a special kind of player in both style and substance. Rich Ashburn's column. Page D3.

Judge lifts ban on abortions with Medicaid

By JANET NOVACK
Bulletin Harrisburg Bureau

HARRISBURG — A Commonwealth Court judge temporarily blocked the state yesterday from cutting off funds for most abortions for poor women. The cutoff was scheduled to begin Saturday.

In issuing a temporary injunction against the funding cut-off, called for in a state law passed last year, Judge John A. MacPhail said pregnant women who receive Medicaid and require "medically necessary abortions" could suffer "irreparable harm" from the law.

The statute bars the state from paying for Medicaid abortions unless the life of the mother is at stake or the pregnancy results from rape or incest promptly reported to authorities.

At present, Medicaid funds also are used to pay for abortions in cases where the mother's health is at stake, a provision that has been interpreted liberally.

Rep. Gregg L. Cunningham (R-Centre), a prime sponsor of the funding cutoff, called MacPhail's ruling the "predictable, inevitable response from the pro-abortion wing of the judiciary."

But, he added, the ruling will merely "forestall the inevitable, and the inevitable is Pennsylvania will not use public

Please see **JUDGE** Page A5

Passing time

Actor Hal Linden and his daughter Nora play a game of cards at Kennedy airport in New York, while waiting for their delayed flight to Israel. Stories of the air traffic controllers strike and its impact appear on Page: A6

AP Photo

Court will appoint city school watchdog

By CHRISTOPHER M. HEPP
Of The Bulletin Staff

Philadelphia Common Pleas Judge Harry A. Takiff announced yesterday that he will appoint a conservator to oversee operations of the Philadelphia School District.

Judge Takiff said he hopes to appoint the conservator within a week. He said that person will be answerable only to the court and serve in the same role as a court-appointed special master or a receiver charged with overseeing "what is essentially an insolvent operation."

That role could include the vetoing of school board decisions if that is deemed necessary, Takiff said.

In his order the judge said the conservator will "make recommendations to this court as to how the resources of the school board can be conserved most efficiently and most prudently to extend the full school year to afford the maximum educational opportunities to the children and to minimize the harm or loss to the discharged employes."

With the possibility of a another school strike looming in September, Takiff said he was appointing a conservator because there is a need to find a "remedy" to the "harm

that this apparently ineradicable annual malady is inflicting."

Takiff also denied a motion by the Board of Education to dismiss a suit by the Philadelphia Federation of Teachers charging the board with breach of contract for ordering the layoffs of 3,500 teachers.

The layoffs were ordered as a means of averting a projected $223-million deficit for the school year that begins in September.

"We have a contract that we are determined will be lived up to," union President John Murray said after Takiff's decision. "We have already set in motion what our actions will be if it is not lived up to."

In ordering the school board to file answers to the complaints raised by the union, Takiff said he doubted that the board could be held to a contract dependent on funding from City Council.

In the same ruling, Takiff dismissed the city, Mayor Green, City Council and its members as defendants in the suit.

"The court has ruled that the city and City Council were not a party to the (contract) agreement (between the school board and the teachers)," City Solicitor Alan J. Davis said, "and the court will not force the city to finance (the agreement)."

PM

TODAY'S BEST BET: The casino industry, which foots the bills for the New Jersey Division of Gaming Enforcement, is complaining about the cost. See Part 3 of Kathy Sheehan's series "Casino People," on Page B7.

WEATHER

Chance of showers and thunderstorms tonight with lows around 70. Partly sunny, warm and a little less humid tomorrow with highs in the upper 80s. (Details on Page D10.)

'Help, I'm drowning!'

Lawyer is saved after his cabin cruiser is cut in half by barge

Bulletin Wire Services

A desperate cry for help led rescuers to a man who swam through the choppy waters of Long Island Sound for 7½ hours after his cabin cruiser sank when cut in half by a barge.

A fisherman pulled Richard Lublin, 41, a lawyer from West Hartford, Conn., from the water about a mile off Orient, N.Y., at about 6.30 A.M. EDT yesterday.

Lublin had apparently swum in the dark, without a life jacket, from the Connecticut side of the Sound, police in Southhold, N.Y., said.

"He was so exhausted he couldn't even lift his head out of the water. What saved him was the change of tide — it pushed him in to the shore," said Reggie Tuthill, the fisherman who rescued Lublin.

On board the cabin cruiser, Lublin said, were his wife, Joan; his daughter, Karen, 9; and neighbors Tom and Rose Markoski and their daughter, Tina, 10. They

all were wearing life jackets when the boat sank, he said.

Air National Guard searchers found Markoski's body at Great Gull Island, between Long Island and Fishers Island, shortly after 3 P.M.

Still missing were Lublin's wife and daughter and Rose and Tina Markoski.

Lublin told the Coast Guard his 36-foot cabin cruiser, the "Karen E," became disabled about 10 P.M. Sunday and was awaiting aid off Westbrook, Conn. After drifting a while, Lublin hailed a passing tugboat for help.

When the tug captain said he could not help and pulled away, the barge he was towing smashed into Lublin's craft, breaking it in half.

The Coast Guard said the tug, the Davy McCallister out of New York, apparently did not realize the severity of the damage to the "Karen E" and radioed the boat suggesting a rendezvous at a buoy about 3 to 3½ miles

Please see **LAWYER** Page A5

Singer Stevie Nicks took a while to get her solo career going, but her fans were willing to wait.

Page C1

INDEX/Tuesday

ATLANTIC CITY B7	LOTTERY A2
BRIDGE D8	OBITUARIES D7
BUSINESS B3	PEOPLE A2
CLASSIFIED ADS C7	PUZZLES D8
COMICS D8	REGION NEWS B1
DEAR ABBY D9	RON GOLDWYN B1
EDITORIALS B8	SANDY GRADY A3
ENTERTAINMENT C1	SPORTS D1
FOCUS C1	TV, RADIO D6
HOROSCOPE D9	WEATHER D10

Nearly everybody reads The Bulletin®

©1981, Bulletin Co. • 133th YEAR, No. 101

The Bulletin

The old gray lady

Nearly everyone "read" The Bulletin

by Craig Ammerman

"Organize the paper and make it more compelling."

The most serious problem we found upon arriving at *The Philadelphia Bulletin* in July 1980 was the way the paper was organized and presented.

The Bulletin's grayness was its most dominant design factor, but that wasn't the only problem. Major features were not anchored. Section fronts often carried advertising. Readers weren't referred to related stories. Information graphics were virtually nonexistent. Those sorts of things.

Over a 10-year period, *The Bulletin's* daily circulation had steadily declined until it had tumbled into a tie with *The Philadelphia Inquirer* at 425,000 copies. *The Inquirer* had a substantial Sunday lead (of more than 300,000 copies), which gave it about 80 percent of the classified dollars. There were other similar nightmares.

But *The Bulletin* had its strengths. It had a comfortable daily lead in home delivery, and this, combined with a solid local news product, allowed it to retain daily leads in retail and food linage. Plus, it was respected by its readers and by much of the community.

Our challenge was to stop the circulation losses, which meant we needed to find out who was ignoring us. Some clue came from my own sophisticated research — hours spent watching people come and go at the major newsstands around the city.

The Inquirer was the choice of young professionals, particularly women (many of whom didn't like either paper). *The Bulletin* seemed to be preferred by persons over 40, certainly by those who were 50 or more. One obvious reason for *The Inquirer's* newsstand success was that it was more compellingly presented. (Gene Roberts, who at the time was editor of *The Inquirer*, might have contended there were other factors as well, but this isn't his space.)

am

As executive editor of *The Philadelphia Bulletin* and managing editor of the *New York Post*, Ammerman has been the senior news executive for the country's two largest afternoon newspapers.

He has held many positions with The Associated Press, including a stint in New York where, as bureau chief and deputy sports editor, he supervised coverage of such major events as the World Series, Super Bowl, Pan American Games and Winter and Summer Olympics, the 1976 Democratic National Convention, and Watergate.

Ammerman is president and co-owner of Health Ink Publishing Group.

The Bulletin

An active sports page

Here's a page that's as active as its content, with a good balance of words, photographs, and graphics — our total news vocabulary.

Words as graphic images

I chose Helvetica as the headline face for its image (the strength of the typeface is suited to the hard-hitting editorial approach) and for its ability to easily turn the news volume up or down, depending on the content. Raymond Lowe designed the logotype for The Bulletin *in 1954. It was the only thing in the paper I didn't change (except to have a bold version cut to support the more active front page).*
R.L.

What we learned

1. *Good packaging is good business.*

It's easier to publish a newspaper that is organized and holds together.

2. *State your goals clearly at the outset and build consensus as you go.*

If you give your staff a clear definition of what you're trying to accomplish and give them the tools (in this case, a flexible design) to do the job, you can go on to the next problem.

When *Bulletin* Publisher Buddy Hayden and I decided to make redesign our first priority, Robert Lockwood was still at *The Morning Call* in Allentown. This would be his first outside consulting assignment.

Our charge to him was: Organize the paper, make it compelling, anchor features and sections, and take the ads off all section fronts. But most important: Create a design that can be adapted to the day's news and, at the same time, make it a design that can be maintained by a news desk that didn't include any modern-day designers. It was this last charge that most concerned me. Based on his work in Allentown, we did not doubt Lockwood's ability to present a beautiful laboratory specimen; my concern was what *The Bulletin* would look like a month after we made the change.

We also hoped to be innovative, to correct some product weaknesses, and to create features and looks that would attract the attention of casual and occasional readers. Some examples of our specific instructions to Lockwood:

The Bulletin

A businesslike approach

We organized the Monday business page with the day of the week and the reader in mind. We gave readers a review of the previous weekend in column one. Column two prepared them for the business week ahead, followed by the local report in column three, national report in column four, and, to complete the picture, a look at future trends in column five.

R.L.

☞ We needed a Monday business page that was different from the pitiful efforts we (and almost everyone else) were publishing then (this was before *The Miami Herald* had a better idea). We told Lockwood we thought the page should have an original, local story; focus on some trends; recap weekend news; look ahead at what might happen this week; and carry graphics highlighting recent market developments.

☞ By this time, it had been a decade since Dave Smith invented the sports agate page. But no Philadelphia paper was doing it very well. What we wanted to do was to anchor the page with a standing feature. Three days a week, it would be a column called "Buck the Bartender," in which we sought to answer the questions sports departments always seem to get late at night from bar patrons. Other days, it was called "Whatever Happened to …" in which we updated the lives of past heroes. Most of our subjects came from reader suggestions.

☞ We were about two years into legalized gambling in nearby Atlantic City; the city's third casino was about to open. The publisher, citing news and advertising needs, felt we should do a daily page, which we did.

3. *Reader participation helps build the newspaper connection with the community.*

Readers can be (probably want to be) contributors. For instance, we found that debate of local issues by local people made a more interesting Op-Ed page; also, we discovered that if you solicit readers as writers with an appealing idea (for example, we asked for stories about "My Favorite Christmas"), you'll get loads of responses and some very readable stuff.

The Bulletin

Style

Frank Lloyd Wright said, "There is a difference between having a style and having style." The word style, in the first instance, is an expression of an individual's personal style — a designer's visual signature. And I suppose in most cases having a style in that sense is fine. I think newspapers are different, and stories should be treated as vehicles of information unfettered by the artist's or reporter's ego (except by recognition with an appropriate use and treatment of bylines). The style should emerge, rather, from a consistent editorial voice.

R.L.

4. *Good work is not always its own reward.*

A design that gives prominence to reporters (bigger bylines, occasional brief biographies on major stories) and columnists (bigger pictures, always anchored) creates identities for the paper. Not to mention what it does to newsroom egos.

We established a local column, ran daily entertainment listings, and published frequent reports on the payoffs at various casinos, etc. And because this was a new page, we used it as the vehicle to introduce the new design.

☞ Our advertising department was moaning about what was happening to it: no more ads on section fronts and no more ads on page 3, which was set aside for national and international news and for the paper's Washington columnist. So, we tried to give them some help on page 2. This was where we would anchor the standard People column and a new daily feature called "One Of Us" — a profile of a local citizen who was leading an exemplary life. The two features, plus standing boxes on what to do if you didn't get your paper, were wrapped around a large standing ad, which was anchored in the upper right two-thirds of the page.

From the examples on these pages, you can judge Lockwood's efforts — and his response to our needs — for yourself. We were thrilled with the results. To be sure, the changes jarred some loyal customers, more than 500 of whom said so in writing ("God didn't give you the right to change

The Bulletin

my newspaper," wrote one). I responded to all of them; six weeks later, we followed up by talking with about 100 of the 500. Three had stopped the paper; we convinced one of them to give us another try.

The design opened the paper so that our editors could present the day's news and their more enterprising efforts to explain those developments in ways that had not been possible before.

Most important, the design held. There were three reasons why it did: (1) Lockwood's design was easy to adapt to the day's developments; (2) Lockwood spent time with each of our desks to help our editors understand how they could make the design work; and (3) our editors worked hard to make it succeed.

And we did win the circulation battle, in that the bleeding stopped. We even had some gains. But … well, you know the rest of the story: *The Bulletin* folded in January 1982. We didn't hold Lockwood responsible for our final chapter.

5. *Enhance both editorial and advertising spaces.*

In certain parts of the paper, it is possible to place advertising in nontraditional locations without doing damage to anybody or anything (above, left).

6. *Recognize your everyday readers.*

If you consistently recognize exemplary, everyday folks (above, right), you'll hear from lots of readers who are threatening to believe you're nice people and who, in the process, give you ideas for future subjects.

Case study three

The Los Angeles Herald-Examiner

LOS ANGELES
HERALD

City/State
Los Angeles, Calif.
Circulation:
Daily: 266,102
Sunday: 289,969
Date of
Implementation:
Design was not
implemented, but parts
were integrated into the
existing paper.
President:
N. S. ("Buddy") Hayden
Design:
Robert Lockwood
Typography:
Body Type:
ITC Garamond
Headline Typeface:
ITC Franklin Gothic
Section Flags:
Futura Bold
Column Logo Typefaces:
ITC Franklin Gothic

LOS ANGELES **HERALD**

The Los Angeles Herald-Examiner
A down-market, hard-hitting broadsheet

by Craig Ammerman

"Organize the paper and bring to it controlled chaos."

In the latter part of 1982, the Hearst Corporation engaged me to read its *Los Angeles Herald-Examiner* for a month. Also, I was instructed to read the *Times* (not the one in New York) and to come forth with some thoughts on what changes the *Herald* ought to consider.

A few months later, Bob Danzig, president of Hearst's newspaper division, and Buddy Hayden, president of the *Herald-Examiner,* summoned Robert Lockwood to a meeting in New York. "Bring Ammerman with you," said Danzig.

There, we were told the *Herald* was going to take a look at up-scale and down-scale options. Lockwood was asked to be the down-scale pilot, with me as his copilot. The charge: Create a tabloid on broadsheet pages. "Be restricted only by the limits of your imagination," said Danzig. It was clear that they wanted an active, down-scale paper, closer to the *Sun* in London than to *Newsday* on Long Island.

It was decided that we would select a one-week period and use actual *Herald-Examiner* editions to create a different paper. We were to produce about 30 section fronts, writing headlines and lead paragraphs based on the news reported by the *Herald* on those days.

A few weeks later, there was another New York meeting. There our initial work was ripped by Danzig and Hayden as being totally lacking in any daring, guts, or innovation. It was suggested that perhaps we simply didn't have any imagination. All we had done was to produce another blue-collar, street-sale paper, they said.

Appropriately chastened, we went in search of new images. As you can see here, Lockwood created some. Probably, you think you know why you've never seen anything like this published in this country. Maybe you're wrong. Certainly the folks in the composing room of the *News-American* in Baltimore, where seven dummy editions with these section fronts were made into mechanicals, or those in the pressroom in Baltimore who printed the editions wouldn't agree. They were fascinated by this approach.

Kate Braverman
Novelist and poet, on Los Angeles: "There is so little tradition here that it lends itself to experimentation. No one's watching for so long that you don't have to worry about taboos. Los Angeles is a new cosmopolitan refugee city for the world. It's a city of confluences. I'm addicted to the metallic, post-apocalyptic sunsets, the Santa Ana blowing through its hot Spanish mouth."

LOS ANGELES
HERALD

Assignment: Create controlled chaos

To turn the news volume up to the level demanded by N. S. Hayden, president of The Herald, *I turned to ideas developed by the constructivist and futurist movements in the 1920s. I tried to retain the energetic immediacy of these earlier forms — their rough-edged vitality — which is frequently lost in the slick corporate designs we see today. Here typography is used as an expressive language as well as a verbal one.*

R.L.

This effort did lead to another. In it, a full newspaper was created, taking a calmer approach to the tabloid-on-a-broadsheet format. This time, Don Forst, who has worked for most urban papers in America, was added to the team. It was surely the only time in Forst's career in which he was brought into something with the specific command to bring sanity and calm to the table.

That effort produced a full broadsheet prototype of about 24 pages, which carried design concepts, proposals for new editorial features and treatments, and revised approaches to some existing features.

While this product proposal was not adopted in its entirety, pieces of it — some new approaches to sports agate, a people feature called "Click," etc. — did begin to appear in the *Herald-Examiner*.

LOS ANGELES HERALD

We think something needs to be said about the sponsor. Bob Danzig and his colleagues at Hearst, in New York and Los Angeles, worked hard and spent much time in search of a solution for their troubled paper. Most others in the business would have surrendered long before. That would have been smart business, we suppose. But it wouldn't have kept the newspaper alive.

Case study four

The Daily News

DAILY◉NEWS

City/State
New York, N.Y.
Circulation:
Daily (a.m.): 1,200,000
Sunday: 1,500,000
Date of
Implementation:
May 1986
Publisher:
James Hoge
Editor:
Gil Spencer
Managing Editor:
James P. Willse
Design:
Robert Lockwood
AME/Graphics:
Thomas P. Ruis
Typography:
Body Type:
Corona
Headline Typeface:
Specially designed
Franklin Gothic Extra
Condensed and Plantin
Section Flags and
Column Logo Typefaces:
ITC Franklin Gothic

DAILY⊡NEWS

The war of the words
Turning the volume up to street level

by James P. Willse

Mirroring the random- ness and complexity of the city.

It was like cleaning out the attic.

After two decades.

No editor or designer had tried in years to sort out the good from the bad from the outdated in the look of the *Daily News.* As a result, the nation's biggest metro had become something of a typeface museum. On any given page, on any given day, readers might be offered headlines in Bodoni, Poster Bodoni, Pabst, Trade Gothic, Helvetica, News Gothic, Spartan, and/or Railroad Gothic, all in a dizzying assortment of heavy and light, roman and italic, condensed and extra condensed.

That wasn't the worst of it. The paper had developed a tired, routine look. The photos in New York's picture newspaper were too small, too predictable. The headlines in a paper known for its headlines (FORD TO CITY: DROP DEAD) looked timid, wimpy. The pages were relentlessly horizontal, modular, boring.

This was 1985, and an outmoded design was something the *News* could no longer afford. The *New York Post* and its cheeky Fleet Street style had built a following with readers (if not with advertisers), and *Newsday* was sending an expeditionary force into New York City armed with process color on the front and back pages.

The Tab Wars were under way, and the *News* needed a bright new look to protect its franchise. Publisher Jim Hoge, Editor Gil Spencer, and I set out to find it.

We turned first to a tabloid genius in England, Sir David English, editor of the stylish and perky *Daily Mail.* English worked up a series of pages that were dynamic and eye-catching but a bit too, well, *English.* There was a lot in the pages that worked. Strongly packaged lead stories, bold use of Franklin heads, great use of double trucks, and a more active, vertical page makeup. But there were British devices that didn't travel well to New York — too wordy readouts, underlining of kickers, heavy use of reverses, and a story count that was too high, creating clutter.

Jim Willse joined the New York *Daily News* as managing editor in 1984 and was named editor and vice president in September 1989.

Willse has been responsible for substantial improvements in the *News*, including its redesign, improved local and sports coverage, and creation of new business, enter- tainment, and women's sections.

After graduation from Hamilton College (Clinton, N.Y.) and the Columbia University Graduate School of Journalism, Willse joined the Associated Press in 1970 as national editor in New York. He was a 1974 Professional Journalism Fellow at Stanford University.

A New York City native, Willse returned to his hometown from California, where he had been managing editor of the *San Francisco Examiner.*

DAILY◎NEWS

Before

*A newspage at war
with its competition
and itself*

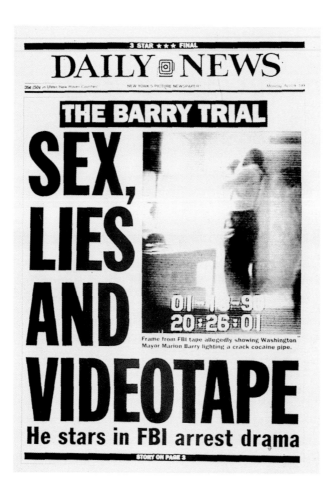

THE BARRY TRIAL

SEX, LIES AND VIDEOTAPE

Frame from FBI tape allegedly showing Washington
Mayor Marion Barry lighting a crack cocaine pipe.

He stars in FBI arrest drama

**Extra, extra,
read all about it.**

*There was a nostalgia in the
newsroom of the New York
Daily News for a newspaper
that never existed in the form
people remember it. We
attempted to capture that ideal
of a popular tabloid using well-
crafted typefaces and a better
organization of news and
advertising spaces. We found
an extra-condensed Franklin
bold for front page headlines to
convey the explosive intensity
needed to sell papers on New
York's cluttered newsstands.*
R.L.

What we learned

1. *Both type and
photos can be
dominant graphic
images.*

**A redesign can and should
be reader-friendly without
losing the tabloid virtue of
impact through strong use
of pictures and headlines.**

2. *One plus one
equals one.*

**Two-page spreads should be
conceived as a single unit,
not as two pages that happen
to fall next to each other.**

The task seemed to be to blend the best of the English approach with the
best of an American tabloid idiom. We turned to Robert Lockwood and
to our resident design genius, Deputy Managing Editor Tom Ruis.

Lockwood retreated to his cave in Pennsylvania, returning a month
later with the first cut of what would become a modernized *Daily
News*. It worked.

The ingredients:
☞New headline faces. Franklin Gothics replaced the old News
Gothics as the main typeface, and the Plantin family became the
secondary type. The result was a more contemporary look that still
felt like the *News* we loved so well.
☞Five-column makeup, rather than four, that gave the design more
flexibility.
☞Moderate use of reverse type, white-on-black and white-on-gray,
that added color (at least the only color *we* were going to have for a
while) to the page.

70

DAILY◉NEWS

**McLuhanism?
Perhaps, but the
medium is the machine**
*"Although completed in 1985
the basic design lent itself to
page makeup on Macintosh
computers. Our front page
design, created on Macintosh
computers using QuarkXPress software, has enhanced the
working relationship between designers and editors.
Because we can do more, more quickly, we make better
decisions later in the news cycle."*
Thomas Ruis

☞ The patented Lockwood grid system, based on the 9.5 point type leading, to help the make-up of the paper.

The most important element of all, and not one that could be codified in a stylebook, was the structural approach to design. Let the news and pictures shape the page, Lockwood preached.

In a way, the *process* was as important as the design, more important than the lines and the type. Lockwood reminded us that information can be conveyed in a variety of ways, and that the story will tell us what tools to use to convey it best to the reader.

Over a period of weeks, the necessary prelaunch steps were taken to implement the redesign. We walked the pages around the newsroom, incorporating the reactions of editors. We formatted typesetting commands and drew new grids on the composing room boards. We got ready.

3. *We're all in this together.*

A successful redesign has to be a grass-roots process, with all parts of the newsroom (and don't forget the composing room) involved. Otherwise, it becomes design-by-fiat and is doomed.

4. *Set clear goals.*

The first step in a redesign is to understand what the paper wants to be. The look of the pages, and how that look is achieved, should reflect the personality of the newspaper.

DAILY◻NEWS

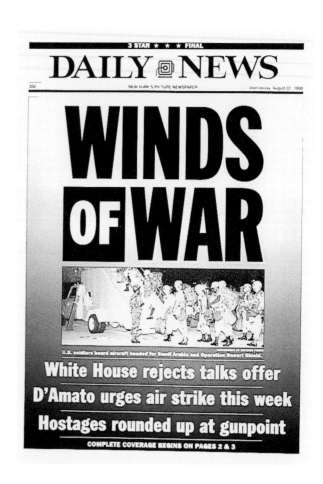

Hard at work
The hard, building-block work of designing is the stripping down of a page to solve a series of visual problems without losing sight of the underlying editorial impetus that is the nut of a good design.
R.L.

5. *Be consistent.*

The elements of the redesign should be consistent throughout the paper. The features section, for instance, can have a distinct feel to it but ought not to look as though it belongs in another publication.

6. *The design is evolutionary — one plane leads to the next.*

Like the paper itself, the design is something of a living document. It needs to be constantly reviewed and freshened. Both the market and the personnel producing the paper change over time.

My litmus test for changes in the *Daily News* is my Uncle Felix DeGregorio, a lifelong News reader now in his 70s. It's rare that we can change a beat assignment or standing head that Uncle Felix doesn't notice.

I waited for his phone call on the first day of the redesign. We had altered the headline type, the shape of the pages, the whole visual attitude of the paper. Would Felix like it?

Finally he called. "What did you do to the paper?" he asked. "We cleaned it up," I said. "How do you like it?" "Not bad. I don't know what it is, but it's got more … *zookety-zook* to it."

Mission accomplished.

Case study five

The Poligrafici Group, Italy

IL TEMPO

Cities
*Rome, Florence, Trieste,
Bologna, and Livorno,
Italy*
Circulation:
*Daily: 800,000
(Combined)*
**Date of
Implementation:**
January 1986
Publisher:
Dr. Andrea Riffeser
Design:
Robert Lockwood
Typography:
Body Type:
Times/Helvetica
Headline Typeface:
*Helvetica Black
Condensed*
Labels, Decks:
Times, Roman and Italic
Section Flags and
Column Logo Typefaces:
Helvetica Extra Bold

IL TEMPO

Florence, Bologna, and Rome

Hardwired for hard news

by Andrea Franchini

The redesign of il Resto del Carlino *(Bologna),* il Piccolo *(Trieste),* La Nazione *(Florence),* il Telegrapho *(Livorno), and* il Tempo *(Rome) is an integral element in an ongoing program of editorial enhancements and technological innovation begun by publisher Dr. Andrea Riffeser in 1985. Additions of new directions in coverage go with changes in the manner in which the news is delivered. A central information center in Bologna produces the international and national news report and delivers it electronically to the other sites, where journalists produce local coverage. Each design is structured to permit information that is electronically delivered.* **R.L.**

Andrea Franchini joined *il Resto del Carlino* as a reporter in 1973. He worked on a 1980 redesign of the newspaper with the Italian newspaper designer Sergio Ruffolo. In 1984 he became chief editor of local pages. In 1985 he was the editorial representative in charge of a project to connect the group's newspapers electronically. Out of this effort a technological news-layout system was developed in-house. Using a Sperry PC-based network, the system connected newspapers in Florence, Bologna, and Trieste. In 1986 Franchini worked with Robert Lockwood on a redesign for the company's newspapers. In 1987 he became "vice directore" of *La Nazione* in Florence and in 1988 "directore" of *Il Telegrafo* in Livorno. In 1989 he left the Poligrafici group to become chief editor of *Il Giorno* in Milan. He now is a free-lance editorial consultant.

First, I must explain that there are important differences between newspapers in my country and those in other countries. The first time Robert Lockwood came to Italy to redesign our newspapers, I presented a small problem: "How can I graphically show the reader that the first lines of this story are *the story* and the following ones are *an interview*?" Robert smiled and said, "It's easy. You write before the story: *This is the story.* And then before the interview: *This is the interview.*"

This kind of thinking and making newspapers is really too American for us. In Italy you simply cannot do it that way. Of course, Lockwood's reply to that is, "Why not?" In the redesign process there were some small and some large problems that Robert tried to resolve in an American way (the most direct, I think). But many times we had to revert to the Italian style of newspapers — trying only to open small windows of futuristic design in the wall of embedded Italian conservatism.

Lockwood also found a similar problem with our production people. Each time he tried to introduce a new solution, they told him: (1) It's impossible; (2) If it is possible, it costs a lot of money; and (3) Even if the owner of the company agrees to pay, it will take a lot of time to do it this way every day. Conclusion: It's impossible!

il Resto del Carlino

Before

A bastion of Italian conservatism

il Resto del Carlino

The 1986 redesign of il Resto del Carlino *is an attempt to create a lively presentation and make the news more accessible to readers. Note the new headline treatment, which consists of labels, bolder heads and decks, summaries accompanying longer stories, windows to the inside, graphics, at-a-glance boxes, briefs, and a better use of photographs.*

R.L.

What we learned

1. *A change in attitudes takes longer than anticipated.*

Like everyone else, journalists are conditioned by outside forces: culture, education, and tradition. They resist change, especially when it appears to threaten their beliefs, lives, and jobs. We need to be more clever and pay more attention to people as we ask them to change their attitudes and adapt to a world of changing readers.

Another thing Lockwood stressed to us is the substantial difference between journalism and communication. Italian journalists may know everything about journalism, he said, but they may know nothing about communicating. And these days, in my country, newspapers compete with television. In recent years, Italian TV has made enormous strides. There are now many new local channels that use a new style of connecting those who are inside the screen with those who are in front of it. Newspapers are not winning this competition. Newspapers are still made as they were 40 years ago. We use the same approaches and have not developed many new ways to connect ourselves to the readers. We use gadgets and prizes to temporarily gain a few new readers. Journalists in our country use Videotels, the National Phone Company's television news service, every day to learn what's going on all over the world. But we don't understand that readers, too, would like to use newspapers as Videotels. So, in Italy, the road toward modern journalism is a very long and bumpy one.

When Robert tried to explain to old-fashioned editors what a new design could be and how images (photographs and graphics) could be used

il Resto del Carlino

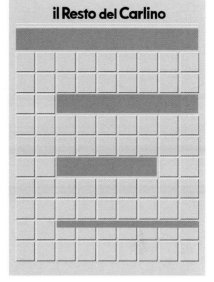

il Resto del Carlino

The front page is produced in Bologna and sent electronically to sites in six other cities. The grid, which was designed by Diego Maver, director of production, corresponds to the templates in the PC system. Using these templates, editors can import reporters' stories to predesignated blocks on the page.
R.L.

effectively, he found resistance. When he suggested that a summary of news on inside pages appear on the front page, he was told that the top left of the front page is untouchable. Italian readers are used to finding only the editor's opinion there. You can see how difficult it is to change not only the design of our newspapers but also the minds of those who produce them.

The same difficulty can be found in attempting to change work environments. Italian journalists are used to working alone; there is a very long corridor between them and production people. Indeed, perhaps it is this remoteness from production that seems to reinforce the journalists' idea that their work is nobler than that of others. Only in the last few years have we begun to use common rooms where journalists work together with production people. Some Italian newspapers have graphics rooms where pages are created, but most still believe that no one other than a journalist can *think* a page. The idea that people who know about journalism and people who know about visual communication can *think a page together* is foreign. Part of the problem may be that in Italy many people still put too much importance on words.

2. *We must think of ourselves as being in the information business, not just simply producing newspapers.*

It's essential to use new technologies, especially microcomputers, to enable us to gather and deliver information more efficiently *and* effectively. By creating a core newspaper in Bologna that produces national, international, sports, and business sections for our newspapers in Florence, Trieste, and Rome, we can better allocate our resources on the local level. Our central graphics agency produces

IL TEMPO

We introduced a better mix of both long and short stories. With longer stories we used chapter heads (he came, he saw, he conquered). Readers don't have to spend 20 minutes looking for the three minutes of information they want.
R.L.

explanatory news packages and graphics, on a Macintosh computer using Quark XPress, and sends them to the other papers in the group. Because the design architecture for all our newspapers is built on the same modular system, we send the packages directly to the information block on the designated page from computer to computer.

3. *Teamwork is the key to better pages.*

In the past we relied on the skills of journalists trained only in writing techniques. They were not educated to think in terms of telling stories visually. We are using our centrally located graphics agency *Polipress* to create teams of journalists

And too many journalists are still producing newspapers for themselves, instead of for the readers.

My former company owns newspapers in Bologna, Florence, Rome, Trieste, Livorno, and Pordenone with a combined global circulation of more than 800,000. Each one has many local editorial offices. So you can buy, for instance, *il Resto del Carlino* of Bologna in 13 different editions. More than 100 pages are offered daily for that newspaper alone. It also has a press agency centered in Rome with foreign correspondents in Paris, London, Bonn, Madrid, Washington, and New York.

New technologies were introduced a few years ago (I was one of the journalists who studied their introduction). Our system comes from Unisys, and we use personal computers with an editorial program of our own. We use Macintosh PCs for information graphics and managing our image database and would like to see their use expanded to pagemaking as soon as possible — we need to stop the quarreling about who shall use them, journalists or production people. (At *il Tempo* in Rome they are

LA NAZIONE

Creating primary signals for each item

The nine-column page creates a newsy look and the opportunity for strong, active vertical layout. We created an agenda page with useful information such as emergency phone numbers, TV highlights, and where-to-go and what-to-do-today information (⦿ 114).
R.L.

exploring the use of QuarkXPress as a pagemaking tool in combination with their Atex system.)

Since the redesign was started, the look of the newspapers hasn't changed much. The process is ongoing. Some of the new ideas have not yet been accepted by editorial people. The point is, as Robert says, we have a final objective in mind, and we are proceeding step by step. Where PCs have been introduced, people have seen how easy they are to use. Our next goal is to change people's minds about new ways of working. Production people must enter editorial rooms, but not as slaves. Graphics people should be welcome inside editorial rooms, imparting all they know about visual communication to those reluctant to accept it.

Working with Robert Lockwood has taught me that there's a moon to explore. And that moon is a place where design means a new way of remaking the old. We're taking it step by step.

who have the skills to gather and package news information.

4. *We must have an overall strategy that encompasses the whole organization.*

We must recognize the complexity of the world and of our organizations. To change to systems better suited to the future, we must change not only our editorial, technological, and business habits, but every aspect of the organization so that all the parts are marching toward the same goals for the benefit of the total organization and not simply for the benefit of an individual part.

The Gazette Telegraph

GAZETTE TELEGRAPH

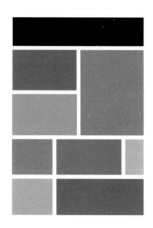

City/State
Colorado Springs, Colo.
Circulation:
Daily (a.m.): 118,577
Sunday: 155,118
Date of
Implementation:
June 1987
Editor:
Tom Mullen
Design:
Robert Lockwood
Typography:
Body Type:
Century Book
Headline Typeface:
Franklin Gothic
Condensed
Section Flags and
Column Logo
Typefaces:
Franklin Gothic Heavy

COLORADO SPRINGS

GAZETTE TELEGRAPH

WEDNESDAY □   SEPTEMBER 21, 1988   ★ 35¢ DAILY 75¢ SUNDAY

COUNTY

Overdue property tax cases up 35 percent

Area's poor economy reflected in increase

By **Joel Millman**/Gazette Telegraph

Another sign of hard economic times in El Paso County was posted Tuesday: The number of properties on which taxes are delinquent is up almost 35 percent this year.

Seven weeks after the Aug. 1 payment deadline, about $10 million in taxes still is owed on 7,740 properties, an increase of 34.7 percent over 1987 when $7 million was owed on 5,745 properties. From 1986 to 1987, the increase was 4 percent.

Deputy Treasurer Ken Kile blamed the area's poor economy for the sharp increase. When people are having cash-flow problems, property taxes take a back seat to car payments, he said.

Property owners who miss the Aug. 1 deadline are subject to penalty charges. If they still haven't paid the taxes and penalties by Oct. 21, a lien against the property is sold at a public auction to recover the delinquent taxes.

Those who fail to pay off the lien, plus 16 percent annual interest, within three years risk losing the property.

All properties on which taxes were delinquent on Aug. 1 will be listed Friday in the weekly Pikes Peak Journal in preparation for the county's annual tax lien sale. This year's auction will be Oct. 23-26 at the Centennial Hall auditorium.

The lien buyer pays the unpaid taxes and late penalties, plus any additional amount he had to bid to win. He gets a lien, or note, against the property.

The property owner then has three years from the date of the sale to pay the lien holder. If the lien, including the 16 percent annual interest, is not paid in three years, the holder has the right to apply for ownership of the property.

Kile said that typically, many of the delinquent property taxpayers will make a tremendous effort to pay their taxes by Oct. 21 to prevent the county from selling a lien against their property.

Overdue real estate taxes in El Paso Co.

Year	Number of properties	Amount delinquent
1986	5,517	$6.3 million
1987	5,745	$6.9 million
1988	7,740	$10.0 million

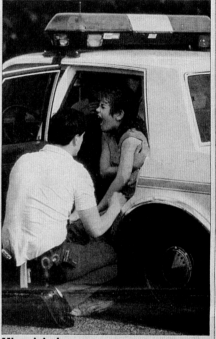

Chuck Bigger/Gazette Telegraph

Minor injuries

Samuel Titus, 11, cries out as A-1 paramedic Ray Blake examines him after the boy was struck by an automobile while riding his bicycle along Chippewa Road in Cimarron Hills late Tuesday afternoon. He suffered only minor injuries in the accident, which was investigated by the Colorado State Patrol.

ECONOMY

GNP growth

Percent change in gross national product from previous quarter, adjusted for seasonal changes and inflation.

Knight-Ridder Graphics Network

Up 3.0%

'85 '86 '87 '88

Change from previous quarter   2nd quarter 1988

Spending on durables   +9.8%
Spending on nondurables   +0.4%
Spending on services   +2.8%
Total personal spending   +3.0%

SOURCE: Bureau of Economic Analysis

Growth, inflation both up during second quarter

Associated Press

WASHINGTON — An improving trade deficit helped economic growth remain strong in the second quarter despite the Farm Belt drought, but inflation was more severe than previously believed, the government reported Tuesday.

The Commerce Department said the gross national product, the broadest measure of the nation's $4 trillion economy, grew at a seasonally adjusted annual rate of 3.0 percent in the April-June period. That was slower than the 3.4 percent expansion rate in the first quarter, but still brisk.

If not for the drought, second-quarter growth would have been a more robust 3.9 percent. Crop and livestock losses for the year are estimated at $13.0 billion and will be even more of a drag on the economy in the third and fourth quarters.

The government said accelerating inflation accompanied the strong growth. One price measure tied to the GNP rose at the fastest pace in nearly six years and was more than triple the first-quarter rate.

The GNP deflator, which reflects changes in buying patterns as well as prices, rose at an annual rate of 5.5 percent in the second quarter, compared with 1.7 percent in the first quarter. It was the biggest jump since the third quarter of 1982.

OLYMPICS

U.S. basketball squad's defense dooms Brazil

Pan Am loss avenged

The U.S. men's Olympic basketball team avenged a Pan Am Games gold medal loss of more than a year ago today in Seoul, South Korea, beating Brazil, 102-87, and showing the defensive pressure that is the trademark of Coach John Thompson's teams.

The United States won its third game of the Olympics by wearing down Brazil and slowing Oscar Schmidt and Marcel Souza, Brazil's outstanding shooters, who combined for 77 points in their country's 120-115 Pan Am victory in Indianapolis. Schmidt had 31 points, but that was nine off his average in Brazil's first two games in Seoul, both victories.

J.R. Reid led the United States with 16 points, 14 in the first half, and Danny Manning and Dan Majerle had 12 each. Souza finished with 11, including only two in the second half. **Complete report/C1**

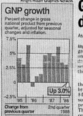

Associated Press

U.S. swimmer Matt Biondi appears dejected after finishing second in the 100-meter men's butterfly final in Seoul, South Korea, Tuesday. West German swimmer Michael Gross is in the background.

U.S. swimmer becomes first triple medalist

U.S. swimmer Matt Biondi, swam to gold and silver, becoming the first triple medalist of the Seoul Olympics Tuesday night (MDT), when he anchored the 800-meter freestyle relay team to a world-record victory over East Germany.

Two hours earlier, Biondi, appearing to let up at the end of the 100-meter men's butterfly, had to settle for the silver medal when Anthony Nesty of Suriname swam past him at the finish to win by .01 of a second. **Complete report/C5**

MILITARY

Service's education under fire

Professional military education is coming under fire from several panels and studies.

The general conclusions are that American officers are good tacticians and able planners and executors of operational plans, but not first-class strategists.

While several changes for military education are being considered, many senior officers believe that officers' careers are already too jammed with requirements. **Complete report/A3**

INSIDE

FOOD
The green tomato has proven it can be as versatile as its ruby red cousin./D1

Freedom Newspapers
Copyright © 1988

WEATHER
Partly sunny and continued warm. High 78, low 52./A2

WORLD

Hamadi beat diver, purser says

Hostage silent during pummeling

New York Times News Service

BONN, West Germany — The purser on a TWA jetliner hijacked in 1985 testified in court Tuesday that the defendant, Mohammed Ali Hamadi, helped to beat a U.S. Navy diver senseless, then ridiculed the American, saying: "Look at him. He thinks he's so strong."

The purser, Uli Derickson, told the court in her first day of testimony that the American, Robert Dean Stethem, suffered the beating by the two hijackers in silence.

"Mr. Stethem was a very courageous man," she said, her voice breaking. "He never made a sound."

"What should this man do? You've beaten him half to death!" she said she shouted at the hijackers.

On the second day of the hijacking, Stethem was shot dead and thrown from the plane, the only fatality of the 17-day hijacking.

Though Derickson testified that Hamadi carried a pistol and the other hijacker grenades, she said she was ordered to the back of the plane during the shooting, and couldn't see who did it.

Since Hamadi acknowledged last month that he took part in the hijacking, but denied that he shot the American, the question of who did the shooting has become one of the central issues in the trial.

Hamadi also claimed that he argued against the shooting and that the other hijacker was the leader.

Former hostages, however, have all identified Hamadi as at least the equal of his comrade in brutality and in authority.

The pilot, John Testrake, further identified Hamadi last week as the murderer, though he acknowledged he did not see the actual shooting.

Derickson also said the hijacker calling himself "Castro," whom she identified as Hamadi, spoke to her longingly in German of his native Lebanon and of a German wife and child, and at **See HAMADI/A3**

Uli Derickson: "Mr. Stethem was a very courageous man"

GAZETTE TELEGRAPH

Telegraphics
Breaking news habits

by John Hutchinson

John Hutchinson graduated from the University of Missouri in 1980. He was a sports reporter for the Sedalia, Mo., *Democrat* and a copy editor for the Jackson, Miss., *Daily News* and the Amarillo, Texas, *Globe-News* before joining the *Gazette Telegraph* in 1981. At the *Gazette Telegraph,* he started in sports as copy editor/reporter and was named assistant sports editor, then sports editor, before he accepted the newly created position of graphics editor in 1985. In 1986 he began work on the complete redesign of the *Gazette* in conjunction with editor Tom Mullen and Robert Lockwood. He was named deputy managing editor in 1987.

Making the message more effective and pleasing

For the staff and management of the *Gazette Telegraph*, the 1990s began in 1986. Freedom Newspapers, Inc. (FNI), the GT's parent corporation, had turned Colorado Springs into a one-newspaper town by purchasing and closing the *Colorado Springs Sun* early in the year. But it was in May of '86 that our vision of the future began to take form.

D. R. Segal, president of Freedom Newspapers, came to Colorado Springs with a challenge from the FNI executive committee: The *Gazette Telegraph,* with the newsroom taking the lead, should immediately begin a major program to become the best newspaper in the 100,000 to 150,000-circulation class in the country.

"They didn't want fine-tuning or window dressing but, rather, fundamental changes," said Editor Tom Mullen. "They wanted us to rethink everything we were doing. They wanted us to get our readers' attention, to be more alive, more fun, and absolutely more useful. They also wanted us to be recognized as a newspaper willing to take risks, to innovate, to really think about our role in the community and our future beyond the next day or next week or even next year. Our goal was to become a newspaper for the 1990s."

Immediately an overall study began. In-house workshops and brainstorming sessions attended by management and staff were conducted. Reader focus groups were well received. Interviews with community leaders and newspaper consultants in the academic and business world were solicited. Newspapers and trade publications from around the world were studied. An effort was made to find newspaper futurists with concrete, more than esoteric, ideas as to what change the '90s would bring.

"That search failed in terms of locating real futurists with solid, practical, hands-on ideas for what the newspaper of tomorrow will be," Mullen said. "We did find some help, but I can't say any concept was really that new. We just brought our own thinking to trends that have been emerging in recent years."

GAZETTE TELEGRAPH

**The design approach
before and after**

The old design (far left) had a generic look. The new design (left) is built on a traditional six-column measure but is laid out as if it were a three-column page. This contributes to an image of the page that reflects the expansive nature of the West and, in particular, Colorado Springs. The ragged-right columns pick up on the informal lifestyle of the city. Information blocks, each with a label, become the building blocks of the page.
R.L.

What we learned

1. *Real change generates paranoia within the newsroom.*

2. *Redesign and major content changes should not be launched on the same day.*

As the study progressed through the summer of '86, priorities for the "New GT" began to take form. We needed:

☞ to meet the information needs of readers who are mostly scanners — the many busy people in a hurry to get the day's news quickly — as well as the needs of other readers with more time or desire for in-depth coverage;

☞ to organize information better for our readers;

☞ to help our readers through the paper;

☞ to improve our writing and produce a tighter, brighter product;

☞ to use methods, such as informational graphics, other than traditional narrative writing to provide information;

☞ to examine the traditional ways of covering news (the beat system) and determine the best method of gathering information for our readers;

☞ to make changes in the structure of the newsroom;

☞ to put color into the paper on a consistent, logical basis;

☞ to change. And that would not come easily or painlessly.

In short, we wanted the "New GT," as we called it, to appeal to our

GAZETTE
TELEGRAPH

Logotype

I incorporated a changing picture postcard into the logotype in an attempt to emphasize the special nature of Colorado Springs. There was a great deal of argument over my suggestions for the flag, above. To my mind, the final compromise, at left, is not a good typographic solution. The prototype fronts also feature a daily news report from the editor and more windows to inside news.

R.L.

changing readership: an information-hungry public that was giving less and less time to their daily newspaper. It had to deliver the information quickly, effectively, and attractively. Above all, we wanted the "New GT" to put readers first, to be a paper that could help them prepare for today, tomorrow, and beyond.

The new design also had to fix the GT's existing problems. Among them were poor organization; sporadic and minimal use of full color; loosely edited, overlong, and uninviting stories; too many say-nothing headlines; and an acute lack of design consistency.

"Not everyone on our staff or in the community welcomes change," Mullen said, "but we are confident the future for newspapers is in finding better ways of meeting reader needs."

Ultimately, we would be judged by our content — the information we would provide our readers. But a redesign of the paper would provide the impetus for our move into the '90s.

3. *Creating a design department is the best way to produce consistent design throughout the newspaper's sections.*

4. *Design for today, but with the ability to adapt to the technological and readership changes of tomorrow.*

GAZETTE TELEGRAPH

From the start, Mullen and I agreed that if a redesign were to be successful, changes in the newsroom structure would be important. We also agreed that an outside consultant, someone who could observe and assist in an impartial way, was needed. We did not want someone who would tell us what type of paper we needed, but one who would help us achieve the paper we believed we needed.

Thus entered Robert Lockwood, who was intrigued by our plans to change the basic approach and structure of the newsroom.

"It was a terrific assignment as far as I was concerned because of the vision and vista that Tom Mullen began with," Lockwood said. "Newspapers tend to make changes without challenging basic assumptions, but what Tom did was go back to the basic ideas of news gathering."

Nothing was more basic than our newsroom structure. We were organized along traditional departments: wire, local, sports, features, business, editorial, photo, and art.

Photo and art were primarily service departments, operating at the direction of editors in charge of the other newsroom areas. Page layout was performed by copy editors, who reported to these same editors. Because these editors had risen through the traditional channels of reporter, copy editor, assistant, and finally department chief, visual presentation — photo, art, and layout — often received a much lower priority than reporting and writing. Indeed, each section of the newspaper reflected that department head's interest and/or knowledge about presenting the news. Clearly, this type of operation would not be conducive to the redesign process.

In 1985, I had been named to the newly created position of graphics editor. In this position, I was charged with directing the photo and art departments, as well as developing a strategy for unifying our presentation of information to the reader. By establishing a photo editor in the newsroom, adding staff to the photo and art departments, and taking our first steps into the Macintosh age, we made rapid and highly visible progress. By the time we began the redesign process, however, we had not been able to build a consistent design philosophy throughout the newsroom.

---

5. *Design is not a one-shot occurrence; rather, it is a continually evolving project.*

6. *Redesign is not a science but an art. It is based on objective fundamentals but requires subjective decisions for implementation.*

7. *Our industry is too resistant to change. It seems to reward imitation rather than innovation. There is a sameness to most papers that reflects insider views. We think the newspaper should be uniquely tailored to our diverse market.*

The redesign was based on a return to basic ideas of news gathering.

GAZETTE
TELEGRAPH

Communities of Interests

Each design should fit its community. When Tom Mullen told me that Colorado Springs grew so rapidly in recent years that it was difficult to identify a particular community, I searched for an image that would reflect this growth. The solution was to replace the concept of geographic communities with one of communities of interests. I saw the city as one composed of different groups, each sharing common occupations, lifestyles, buying patterns, and interests. For example, the military constitutes one such community. A story on Pentagon spending gets a large readership. Instead of a labeling strategy targeted solely to geographical communities, we designed one for communities of interests as well (⊙ 31).
R.L.

Upper management agreed that a structural change was needed. A design department was the result. We looked at creating a universal design desk but rejected this idea on the theory we would be establishing another entity dedicated to establishing turf and defending it against outside influences. We wanted to avoid this traditional method of operation.

We wanted to integrate design into the newsroom process, making sure the content of each section was presented in a manner that would interest and induce readership. To do this, we set up a 10-person team. Page designers operate at each content-originating desk, working with the slot person responsible for the content of the section.

"The page designers are working partners with the city desk, the sports desk, the news desk, the business desk, and the features desk," Mullen said. Each desk has a somewhat different way of operating, and designers adapt to those methods while maintaining the overall consistency of our design. They report to a design director, who has the responsibility

GAZETTE TELEGRAPH

Color

There is a difference between a colorful page and one that uses color well. On these pages the content, photographs, graphics, and labels deliver the color. There is no attempt to "colorize" the page.
R.L.

and the authority to maintain overall continuity and consistency in the paper's design from front to back, across all sections.

Page designers are responsible for the layout of every news page except the editorial pages, which are highly formatted and handled by the editorial department. Design work is critiqued daily, and brainstorming sessions encompassing the entire group are often held.

"The designers get a lot of feedback," deputy managing editor Terri Fleming said. "That's something we never had before. It had been a lonely job."

As page designers became accepted in the newsroom, we also envisioned them bridging the visual gap that often exists between editors and photo/art. In a way, each designer would become a department graphics editor, a person who would understand the importance of story play and could discuss the graphic possibilities with the visual department, helping eliminate wasted assignments, duplication of effort, and the lack of visuals with stories that demand them.

GAZETTE
TELEGRAPH

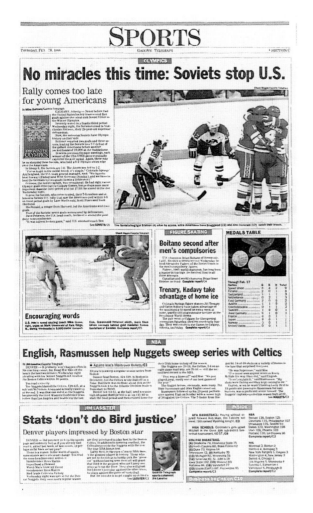

Once we were comfortable with this newsroom structure, we began reorganizing the paper's content. We were asking for extensive color fronts and at the same time we wanted to anchor as many of our sections and features as possible, thus allowing readers immediate access to their favorite part of the paper. This required close coordination and cooperation with advertising and production.

Our initial idea was to provide a four-section daily paper with the first section dedicated to local, national, and world news and editorial pages; the second section to sports and business; the third section to classified advertising; and the final section to features, including comics.

Owing to press configuration and fluctuations in advertising, we were unable to achieve our preferred setup. With the publisher's backing and the support of circulation, advertising, and production, we were guaranteed a minimum of four full-color fronts each day and a consistent flow of wire news, local news, sports, business, and lifestyle. This flow allows us to plan and organize each section better and provides scanners

GAZETTE
TELEGRAPH

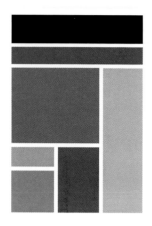

Layout

The layout blocks give the editors the flexibility to let that day's news report determine the shape of the stories and the design of the pages (⊙ 22).
R.L.

with a quick-to-recognize, easy-to-devour format. At the same time the format affords us the room for display that is needed for in-depth work.

Once we had completed our research, determined our structure, and decided how we wanted to organize the product, it was time to begin the redesign process, working out all the details to the point of launch. With the advance work we performed and extensive information we had available, it was neither an especially difficult nor a time-consuming process. We were well prepared, and the design began to take form immediately.

Highlights of what was incorporated include anchored section fronts; expanded use of full and spot color; four section covers guaranteed color on a daily basis; a bigger business section; a consolidated lifestyle section; shorter, tighter stories; high-information headlines; fewer jumps (shooting for a maximum of one per cover); the use of story capsules on the cover pages to better serve scanner readers; more reference/index material; story/package labeling; and better display of good photography.

GAZETTE
TELEGRAPH

The new design gave the paper quick solutions to the organizational, color, and visual problems. Creation of a design desk quickly solved the consistency problem.

But achieving the content changes — tighter editing, high-information headlines, fewer jumps, shorter stories, and capsuled stories — was more difficult and encountered more staff resistance. It took more time, but progress was made. And the process continues. Change, we have discovered, is not a one-giant-step process; rather it is an ongoing series of small steps of continual education and experimentation that should take us to our ultimate goal.

Case study seven

The London Free Press

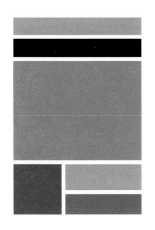

City/State
*London, Ontario,
Canada*
Circulation:
*Daily (a.m.): 118,577
Sunday: 155,118*
**Date of
Implementation:**
January 1989
**President,
Assoc. Publisher:**
James Armitage
Editor:
Philip McLeod
Design:
Robert Lockwood
Art Director:
William McGrath
Typography:
Body Type:
Imperial
Headline Typeface:
Franklin, Caslon
Section Flags and
Column Logo Typefaces:
Franklin, Caslon

FIRST MINISTERS' CONFERENCE
 New hope for the Meech Lake Accord/Pages A8,10

WEEKEND

The London Free Press

CITY EDITION · SATURDAY, *November 11, 1989* · NEWSSTAND PRICE 75¢

Fifty years ago today, on Nov. 11, 1939, a huge crowd gathered at the cenotaph in London's Victoria Park. The snowflurries that morning could not white out humanity's blackest truth – the world was again at war against Germany. The world is once more witness to dramatic events in the two Germanys. A hole has been punched in the Berlin Wall – the Iron Curtain that symbolized a war that never seemed to end. There's renewed hope this Remembrance Day morning that Nov. 11, 1989, truly will be ...

THE EAST BLOC IN TRANSITION

A DAY TO REMEMBER

ON PAGE A2
❑ East Germany punches holes in the Berlin Wall for new border crossings and permanently lifts travel restrictions on its citizens. About 300 East Germans watch in amazement as civilian building workers move in to help border troops begin removing a section of the wall.
❑ West German Chancellor Helmut Kohl tells thousands of cheering Berliners that West and East Germany belong together and must work for a common future.
❑ The Soviet Union blesses the dramatic opening of the Berlin Wall, but a leading foreign ministry spokesman emphasizes that reunification of the Communist and capitalist Germanys is not in the cards as long as the separate East and West military alliances exist.

ON PAGE A3
❑ An estimated 100,000 East Germans pour into West Berlin and enjoy their new-found freedom by partying it up.
❑ A London woman was in West Berlin the day the wall started going up. "If I were in Berlin right now, I would be dancing on the wall with the rest of them ... It's a whole new age," she said.
❑ A former Londoner who works at Canadian Forces Base in Lahr, West Germany, says none of the East German refugees flooding in will be housed at the base, despite earlier reports.

ON PAGE A4
❑ In Bulgaria, Todor Zhivkov resigns after 35 years as Communist party leader in which he led his country through the Cold War and made it an impenetrable part of the Iron Curtain.

ON PAGE A5
❑ Solidarity leader Lech Walesa declares a new era is dawning in Europe.
❑ The secretary-general of NATO says the prospects for ending the division of Germany and Europe have never been better now that the East German border has been opened.

East and West Berliners stand on the Berlin Wall in front of the Brandenburg Gate Friday after East Germany opened its borders to the West.

Associated Press

Images of war and peace: a special poem
Today we remember the sacrifices of veterans with a specially commissioned poem by James Reaney and Colleen Thibaudeau, a visit to the birthplace of John McCrae, who wrote the poem In Flanders Field, and a reflection on a generation that hasn't known war. **Encounter**

Our readers recall their war experiences
In September we invited readers to tell us their experiences and memories of the war. Some are poignant, some shocking, all insightful. A military nurse recounts the touching battle to save a wounded child; an East Ender recalls the bombing of London, England; a teenager remembers life in Hitler's Germany; and many more. **Pages A6-7**

Underground bunker set for Armageddon
Bruce Beach of Horning's Mills, near Mount Forest, believes the Third World War is inevitable — and he's ready for it, with 42 school buses forming an underground bunker for the first 500 arrivals. **Page F1**

THE BEGINNING ... AND THE END

The week's tumultuous events in East Germany, where border controls were dropped and free elections promised, drew these comments:

❑ **West German Chancellor Helmut Kohl:** "The spirit of freedom now reigns all over Europe — Poland, Hungary, and now, East Germany. We claim this right for all people in Europe. We claim it for all Germans. "We are and will remain one nation and we belong together. ... Step by step we must find the way to our common future."

❑ **East German leader Egon Krenz:** "We have a great task before us, a revolution on German soil, which will bring us a socialism that is economically effective, politically democratic, (and) morally clean."

❑ **Prime Minister Brian Mulroney:** The opening of the wall is "one of the most powerful statements" possible about the strength of democracy, individual courage and the desire for freedom. "It was very moving" to watch TV clips of East Germans chipping away at the wall, Mulroney said. "They're very courageous people and deserving of all our support. I salute them for their courage."
❑ **President George Bush:** He said the developments in East Germany will give his meeting in Malta with Soviet President Mikhail Gorbachev in December "even more importance." The changes in the East bloc "make clear that the process of reform initiated by the East Europeans and supported by Mr. Gorbachev and by Americans and by our allies is real."

❝ From Stettin in the Baltic to Trieste in the Adriatic an iron curtain has descended across the continent. ❞
— Winston Churchill,
Britain's wartime prime minister
March 5, 1946

❝ Democracy has won the political battle, the market has won the economic battle, the Cold War is finished. ❞
— Arthur Schlesinger,
Key adviser to President John Kennedy,
Nov. 10, 1989

WEATHER

Windy, chilly
High of 6, low of 2
Details on Page C11

INSIDE

FRONT SECTION
Lottery check /A2
National news /A8,10,12
World news /A4-5,11
SPORTS/BUSINESS
Jim Kernaghan /B1
Racing /B6
Scoreboard /B6
Business, markets /B8-14
LONDON & REGION
Morris Dalla Costa /C1
Deaths, births /C10-11
Weather /C11

OUR TIMES
Ann Landers /D8
Birds /D11
Books /D12
Bridge /D9
Chess /D14
Comics, crossword /D13
Horoscope /D10
Family notices /D10
Science /D11
Stamps /D4
TV listings /D4
CLASSIFIED /E1-20
Wheels /E3

FORUM
Editorials, letters /F2-3
Instant Replay /F5
Churches /F6-7
TRAVEL
Since You Asked /G7
HOMES
Let's Decorate /H9
You Wanted to Know /H14-15
Gardening /H12
Video /H16
Classified ads /H17-48

Plus: Comics, Encounter

The London Free Press

Reinventing the newspaper

"What the hell have you done to my paper?"

by Philip A. McLeod

"On the days when it works, it's a reader's newspaper."

The telephone rang shortly after noon. A woman, identified only as between the ages of 35 and 45, married with two children and working outside the home, was calling about the new design of *The London Free Press.*

She had called earlier, she explained, back a month before when the morning newspaper first adopted its new look — a design that was clearly aimed at her if at anyone in particular. But the first morning she saw the new design she hadn't liked it, she said, and had called the newspaper to complain.

Now she had changed her mind. She was getting used to the colorful front-page road map, to the graphics, to the learning boxes, to summary paragraphs, and to shorter narratives. In fact, she just wanted someone to know that now that she was more familiar with the paper, well, "I love it," she said.

After a month of scores of letters and hundreds of telephone calls — some thoughtful, many abusive, most critical — it was damn nice to finally hear from a fan. To the editors of the first Canadian daily to enter Robert Lockwood's world of newspaper presentation for the 1990s, that day in early March was a much-celebrated turning point.

But that's getting ahead of a story that had started more than two years earlier when senior managers of *The Free Press,* Canada's largest privately owned daily, launched an ambitious make-over to better satisfy reader needs.

The make-over project, scheduled to be completed by the end of 1989, was dubbed "The Newspaper for the 1990s." Before it was finished, it would involve more than 100 people, cost one editor-in-chief his job, and force a massive reorganization of newsroom operations. Indirectly, it would lead to editorial employees joining The Newspaper Guild, the first union in the newspaper for more than 30 years. It would also cause a widespread and, at times, acrimonious debate within the Canadian newspaper industry over the most appropriate way of winning back readers.

Born in Winnipeg, Manitoba, son of a Baptist minister, Philip McLeod was raised in Nanton, Alberta, a small (pop. 1,000) farming community 60 miles south of Calgary. He got into the newspaper business by starting his own paper at age 15. He went professional in 1962 with *The Herald-Tribune* in Grande Prairie, Alberta. Grande Prairie was, at that time, the last place in the country where homesteading was possible, so both the town and the paper had a strong pioneering spirit.

He won a Southam Fellowship for Journalists and a year at the University of Toronto in 1970–71 before becoming publisher, at age 28, of the *Truro* (Nova Scotia) *Daily News.*

In 1976 he moved to the *Toronto Star*, Canada's largest newspaper, as a copy editor, later working as a political reporter, national editor, senior news editor, and deputy managing editor. He became editor of *The London Free Press* in 1987.

The London Free Press

Before

*Both design and
content are well
behaved and polite.*

A user's manual

*One-half to three-quarters of
the front page consists of
summaries in words, pic-
tures, and graphics of the
most interesting information
inside the paper. On the top
half of the page are more
traditional packages. Each
story package has a subject
label, headline, summary,
narrative with chapter
heads, and, when possible,
an at-a-glance box. The
facade of the front page is
not only a billboard, a
simple sign, but also a
complex intimation of much
more within.*

R.L.

What we learned

1. *News is what
readers want most.*

**A redesign should
emphasize the importance of
the rigorous and vigorous
practice of good journalism
in every section, on every
page, through every story in
the paper.**

2. *People want to
know about people.*

**A redesign should mark a
shift away from institutional
news coverage toward
stories that tell how
news affects people, as
individuals, as groups, as
communities.**

None of that, of course, was known — or even expected — when James Armitage, the company's president and associate publisher, brought in Chris Urban, a highly respected market researcher from the United States, to find out what readers thought of *The Free Press* — and, more to the point, why they were leaving.

On the surface, the newspaper was a fat cat. *The Free Press* is the only daily published in London, a rapidly growing and prosperous city of 300,000 known for its world-class medical facilities, large university, and diversified financial and manufacturing base. London is the distribution center for southwestern Ontario, a region of nearly 750,000 people nestled at the bottom of Canada along a freeway halfway between Detroit and Toronto. There are six local daily papers in the region, three television stations, and outside competition from five Detroit and Toronto metro dailies. But none has the reach or the clout of *The Free Press,* which in 1989 celebrated its 140th year.

By 1987, *The Free Press* circulation averaged 130,000 six days a week, up 20,000 since the mid-'60s. What caused the company concern, however,

The London Free Press

was that household penetration in the two-decade period had dropped from 95 percent to 60 percent — and was still dropping. And recently, total circulation had begun to decline as well.

Urban's survey of 1,500 residents of London and the five-county region surrounding the city, presented to senior managers in January 1987, was tough. "Readers perceive the newspaper as well-written, well-organized, and professionally produced," Urban wrote, "but many believe it misses important local stories, has a poor understanding of community issues, is not written for people like them, has few interesting articles, and is relatively dull." Urban also found, as have several studies since, that time constraints were increasingly a factor behind dwindling readership.

First casualty of the research was the editor-in-chief, who had been at the paper nearly 30 years. Many argued at the time he was unfairly made the scapegoat for a management system that bred complacency. James Armitage, who had joined *The Free Press* two years earlier, responded by noting that the editorial department, also surveyed by Urban, had been

3. *Explain what you are doing and why.*

You can never tell your staff — or your readers — often enough what you are doing and why. We found that readers and most staff weren't paying attention when we were explaining the redesign, and we had finished explaining when they began to pay attention.

4. *Take enough time to do the job properly.*

Have a deadline but don't be in too much of a hurry. It's better to learn to do a few things very well than a lot of things rather poorly.

The London Free Press

even harder on the newspaper than readers. It was time, he said, for new leadership.

After a four-month, cross-Canada search, *The Free Press* announced in mid-October 1987 that Philip McLeod, senior deputy managing editor of *The Toronto Star,* had been hired as the new editor. Three months later, in a two-paragraph item in *Editor & Publisher* magazine, it was announced that Robert Lockwood had been engaged to assist with a redesign project. The drive to create The Newspaper of the 1990s had begun.

Task Force for Revolution: Sitting in his small, cluttered office in a corner of *The Free Press* newsroom, Richard (Dick) Ward hardly looks the part of a revolutionary. A conservative dresser, his graying hair slicked straight back, Ward as managing editor was capping a 35-year career when he was picked to head the small newsroom study group that would be the force behind the redesign project. He would admit later he was reluctant to take the job; he had already decided to retire once the new editor was in harness. But, convinced the project offered a challenge to create something really new, he saw it as the perfect ending to his 35 years at the newspaper.

To round out the task force, Ward picked George Kemick, assistant news editor; Bill McGrath, graphics coordinator; and Jane Foy, a feature writer who was serving a one-year stint as assistant assignment editor. They were an unlikely but, as events would show, an inspired foursome — Kemick, a sharp, aggressive editor with traditional newspaper tastes; McGrath, a founding member of the Society for Newspaper Design, whose talents as a designer had long been underused; Foy, a bubbly personality with eclectic tastes equally at home with scientists and reggae musicians; and Ward, careful by nature and a leader by consensus.

Their first meeting was hardly encouraging. They had trouble agreeing on priorities and procedures. McGrath, who had been preaching the need for better design for a decade, recalls thinking that the paper had missed many trends in design, "… I was faced," he said, "with the prospect of having to do something I might not like." But he saw the agenda as "elegant type, handsome logos, a color policy that would take us from the circus-poster school to an effective art of communication, and tons of information graphics."

The London Free Press

The news in sharp relief

News rises from the page at different speeds to different levels. For example, color and primary signals such as graphics rise to the reader's eyes quickly, while text rests on the surface of the page. One should be aware of this extra dimension — like looking at a sculptured surface — when designing the page (◉ 115).

R.L.

To Kemick, it was like a "rooster dance with everyone strutting his own point of view. I recall sitting there looking at an artist, a reporter, and a managing editor, wondering how the hell we were going to put together a realistic redesign when the realities of their individual jobs and perspectives weren't, in my view as a deskman, the realities that it took to put out a daily newspaper on deadline."

Whatever their differences, the foursome did agree Lockwood was the best choice as their design consultant.

Everyone associated with the redesign project had second thoughts about Lockwood when he paid his first visit to London early in March 1988. Although editorial staff had been more critical of the newspaper than readers, there was less than overwhelming support for redesign — or, at least, for the direction redesign was now widely predicted to take. The newsroom rumor mill had it that *The Free Press* would soon look exactly like *USA TODAY*. Lockwood didn't exactly put the rumor to rest, either. Answering one question from a roomful of unsure

5. *Show and tell.*

You need to promote the redesigned newspaper heavily and for an extended time. The merits of the new product are not self-evident to those who no longer regularly see it.

The London Free Press

Newsroom strategies

Designing a news page requires not only editorial insight but also the ability to marshal the newsroom resources required to deliver a comprehensive and comprehensible report. In other words, it requires teamwork among different disciplines.

R.L.

6. *The importance of the link between staff organization and the resulting product.*

A redesign project will almost inevitably also require some dramatic changes in management style and newsroom organization. The likelihood of this should not be underestimated, nor should the difficulty of actually making the necessary changes.

journalists that rainy morning, he didn't rule out a *USA TODAY* look, if that's what the newspaper wanted. Or a *Wall Street Journal* look, either. The content of a newspaper, he said, should determine its design.

That was the message Lockwood continued to preach in his first meeting later that day with the redesign task force. "You have to decide what you want to put into the newspaper," he said. "Then, and only then, should you worry about what it looks like." He urged an in-depth study of content — what was in the paper and what should be in the paper — before any work was done on creating its new look.

Ward has often acknowledged since that the content study, an exercise that would take nearly four months to complete, was perhaps the most important step toward creating a newspaper that was truly designed for readers. It was also an unexpected opportunity to involve many more journalists in the redesign process. The task force was expanded by 12 people and each was asked to form a subcommittee to study a specific content area. The front page, national and international news, local and regional news, the editorial page, the Op-Ed page, sports, business, lifestyle, entertainment, business, the weekend magazine, the Monday business magazine, the new homes

𝕿𝖍𝖊 𝕷𝖔𝖓𝖉𝖔𝖓 𝕱𝖗𝖊𝖊 𝕻𝖗𝖊𝖘𝖘

section, the travel section, daily and weekend comics, and syndicated features — all came under scrutiny. In establishing the committees, Ward set down three rules: No chairman would critique a section of the paper for which he or she worked; nothing in the paper was sacred, no idea too outrageous; and minutes had to be kept of each meeting and posted in the newsroom. For more than a month the newsroom buzzed, the discussions often spilling across the street to the Press Club bar.

By mid-April, the redesign task force was meeting daily with the content subcommittees, sorting through hundreds of ideas in search of the consensus that would shape their report to the editor. And early in May a red-bound binder that would set the newspaper on a new course was circulated to senior managers.

The content study contained 321 specific recommendations for deletions, changes, or additions. Among its main proposals: A repackaging of *The Free Press* into five sections with consistent, anchored features each day; a new omnibus lifestyle and entertainment section to be called "Our Times"; a page-one road map to major stories inside; a stronger emphasis on people stories and a corresponding reduction of political coverage; broader sports coverage that would in particular accentuate local events; a new weekend section of commentary and analysis; and the use of new storytelling tools, in particular, graphics and summaries.

In its summary of the content study, the task force described the new direction for the paper: "Our recommendations incorporate three themes intended to make *The Free Press* an essential service in our community, to make it indispensable to people living in an Information Age: (1) News is what readers want most. The redesign should emphasize the importance of the rigorous and vigorous practice of good journalism in every section, on every page, through every story in the paper. (2) People want to know about people. The redesign should mark a shift away from institutional news coverage toward stories that tell how news affects people, as individuals, as groups, as communities. We want to personalize the news. (3) Regional news offers the best chance for growth. Our readers want to know what's happening, not just in their backyards, but in their 'whole neck of the woods'.

The general feeling around *The Free Press* was that the recommendations, taken in total, made sense. But when individual editorial department heads contemplated what was proposed for each of their sections, there was less agreement. Now another facet of the Lockwood plan came to the fore: Unless persuasive arguments could be

7. *There is no such thing as too much training.*

What is needed, however, are innovative hands-on training sessions in which the trainees are really involved rather than acting as passive bystanders. In-house training is more effective (because it's more real) than seminars far away. A training program needs to be ongoing.

8. *The redesign is the beginning, not the destination.*

The really successful redesign project never ends. The process must be self-critical and, therefore, constantly evolving.

The London Free Press

made to the contrary, the answer to any question raised was, "Yes, we can." That laid vested interests and years of "we've always done it that way" to rest. By the end of June the content study had been accepted. Whatever happened next, *The Free Press* would never be the same again.

Something old, something new: July 1 is a national holiday in Canada, the day the country marks its founding in 1867. But it wasn't a day off for *The Free Press* redesign task force, which celebrated Canada's birthday with California wine and a good meal at a quaint little restaurant near Robert Lockwood's home outside Allentown, Pa. Phase Two of their project was under way — and it wasn't going well. The group was split on the direction the new design should take. McGrath the artist and Foy the freethinker wanted something that would really show the folks back home. Kemick, burned once before at another newspaper by a redesign that got too far ahead of readers, urged caution. As chairman, Ward sat on the fence, but he was mindful that whatever direction they went, he would have to sell it to his boss. The argument continued late into the night and arose again the next day at Lockwood's office.

The London Free Press

Lockwood told the group he would help them design whatever they wanted but, he kept pressing, the content study showed clearly the newspaper was prepared to break new ground. Now was the chance. Shortly after lunch, while the Canadian visitors were taking a breather, Lockwood called back to London. He had only one question: "How far do you want me to push your people?" As far as possible, he was told. Back with the task force he offered a compromise solution — why not try several alternatives, one more traditional and another more progressive. It worked — and by the time the week in Allentown was over, the traditional had blended into the progressive. The four versions of Page One the task force brought home to London were like nothing else seen before in a daily newspaper anywhere in Canada.

The top half of the page retained a somewhat traditional look — regular headlines and two stories in narrative style. Accompanying each story package was something new — a summary of its contents. Below the fold, however, the page was a kaleidoscope of color — summaries in words, pictures, and graphics of the most important and interesting information inside the paper. Eventually the summaries would be color-coded to match the logos of the newspaper's sections. Lockwood had clearly pushed the task force.

Behind the prototypes was a concept for a newspaper aimed at winning busy readers, but one that did not sacrifice the strength of print journalism — depth and substance. A host of new storytelling techniques were to be introduced — labels and summary decks, graphics and lists of background facts, questions and answers, breakouts of quotes to show opposing views. A high prize was placed on multiple entry points to story packages so that more content was exposed. The idea was that readers in a hurry could skim through story packages quickly, but the detail was also there for readers who wanted more (⊙ 114).

When the Page One prototypes went up on the newsroom bulletin board in early August, the staff was clearly split. Reporters felt threatened, partly because a front with only two stories reduced their opportunity to make Page One and partly because the prototypes seemed to foretell a move to shorter stories. Editors, on the other hand, were more inclined to support the concept, but they worried about all the extra work it seemed to suggest.

Whose paper is it anyway?
"To attract busy readers, it was often appropriate and necessary to break long narratives into parts for a story package. The most important consideration was how much information a reader could get and how much time that would take."
Philip A. McLeod

103

The London Free Press

During a series of staff meetings in late summer, Kemick and Foy fought to convince their colleagues. As an editor, Kemick explained that stories weren't something that only reporters prepared. For readers, he said, the story was a combination of all the elements in a package, including headlines, artwork, summaries, lists of important facts, background breakouts, and narrative. To attract busy readers, it was often appropriate and necessary to break long narratives into parts for a story package. The most important consideration was how much information a reader could get and how much time that would take. And Foy, the reporter, offered nervous editors this illustration of how the newspaper's resources could be stretched to handle the extra work the new design implied: "We'll be able to do this," she deadpanned, "because we won't be doing a lot of other things anymore."

The future starts today: By mid-September, when the newspaper's senior managers met to approve the project, it was too late to turn back. Lockwood's notion that the answer was "Yes, unless," was now a tidal wave sweeping opposition aside. Other newspaper departments were infected, too, and long-standing constraints were eliminated. The production department found a way to print the new "Our Times" section as part of the live press run. Advertising agreed to block layout and to give up some color positions. Circulation and promotion departments geared up to capitalize on the attention the new design would create.

With virtually no debate, the design was approved and a launch schedule established. *The Free Press* would enter the 1990s over a four-month period, one section at a time, with the new front page and all the accompanying bells and whistles to make their debut on Jan. 30, 1989. Despite the skeptics — and there remained many — the newsroom was committed to the project. But it was clear that a sweeping reorganization would be necessary to reallocate resources to the task. Three new departments were created. One, headed by Kemick, pulled together all the news page designers and graphic artists. A second, headed by McGrath, grouped all the feature page designers. And a third, headed by Foy, joined lifestyle and entertainment writers and editors. Other changes saw the appointment of a weekend editor, a new city editor, and a new sports editor.

Meanwhile, the task force launched training programs for editors and reporters during the daytime and then labored long into the night to complete prototypes for interior pages. Everywhere there was confusion

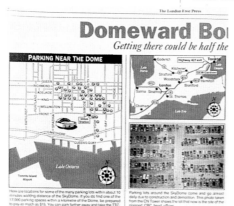

Maps

No map is entirely accurate. It is an abstraction. In Barry Lopez's phrase, it is the "projection of a wish that the space could be this well-organized," where spaces are turned into places. Maps masquerade as authorities.

R.L.

The London Free Press

and chaos — even some last-minute second-guessing about the launch schedule from the personnel department, which worried that longtime employees were being left behind.

On Monday, Oct. 31, 1988, the new entertainment and lifestyle section, "Our Times," appeared for the first time in *The Free Press,* complete with many of the redesign features. And on the following Saturday, the new "Forum" section of opinion and analysis joined the package. Community reaction was subdued, despite the beginning of a four-month promotional campaign that was to be the most expensive and aggressive in the newspaper's history. In early December, the combined sports and business section made the switch. There was a little more fuss from readers, but most seemed preoccupied by the pre-Christmas rush. In early January, the local news section was redesigned, followed a week later by the weekend homes and travel sections.

Then came Monday, Jan. 30. Now it was all out there. In a front page note to readers, Ward explained what had been happening down at the newspaper office for the past year. He listed the new design elements, underlining once again how these were aimed at helping busy readers get information quickly. He described how the paper's news agenda was changing, putting the emphasis on useful and timely and relevant rather than merely yesterday. Tell us what you think, he said confidently at the end of his note: Phone this number.

The phone lines opened at 8 a.m.; the first call rang in a minute later. "What the hell have you done to my paper?" a long-time subscriber yelled. He wasn't alone. More than 600 people called the first day, nearly 300 the second. More than 1,100 in all the first week. Three-quarters didn't like it, especially the front page. "Your paper looks like *USA TODAY*," one caller said. *"The National Enquirer,"* said another. Or a comic book. Or a preschooler with new crayons. But ever so slowly the tide turned over the next few weeks. Finally came the call from the woman who had changed her mind.

And in May, for the first time in two years, the paper recorded a year-over-year circulation increase — 12 copies. That it was all necessary remains the firm conviction of those most closely associated with the project. That it was worthwhile remains the fervent hope of the entire staff. In hindsight two valuable lessons were learned for the next time. The first is to take enough time to do the job properly and then add a little more to think it all through again. The second is to redesign the people in the newsroom first, then redesign the newspaper.

Sky Dome insert

After 2½ years of construction, the Sky Dome with its retractable roof was scheduled to open to the public with a gala celebration on Saturday, June 3, 1989.

In London, Ontario, in the summer of 1989, amidst the daily struggle to make sense of a constantly changing world, the redesign of *The Free Press* and the people who shape it continues. There are fewer meetings now; Lockwood doesn't call as often, and Ward is packing his stuff away for retirement. Out in the newsroom, reporters offer suggestions for graphics and write fact boxes without being asked. But they call it an editor's newspaper now.

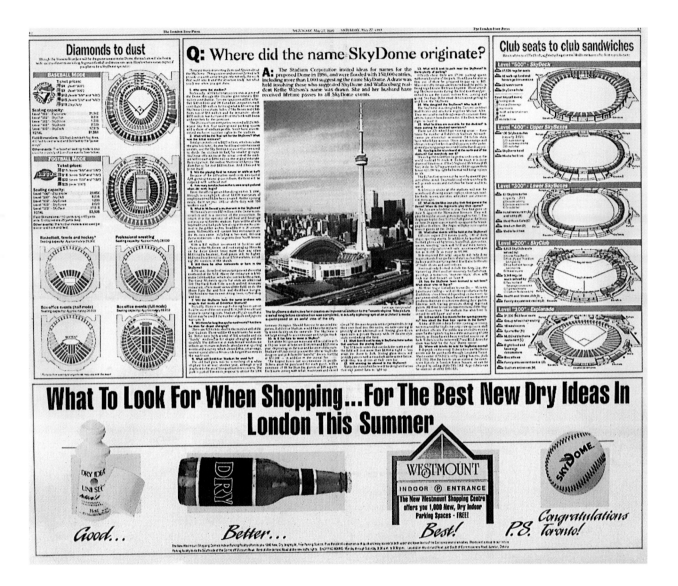

It's not really that. On the days when it works, it's a reader's newspaper. Ward knows. Returning home from a trip, he tries to hail a cab at the airport. The driver pays no attention; he's too busy reading the paper's special section — all graphics — on the new domed stadium in Toronto.

George Kemick, the editor in charge of the front section, got together with artist Trevor Johnston to plan this insert. Johnston toured the Dome and compiled this comprehensive look at Toronto's modern-day colosseum.

Section four

Art of change

*The reader, the newspaper, the organization,
and the journalist*

The reader

"Take back this pudding, it has no theme."
Winston Churchill

The world is watching America and America is watching TV.
Bumper sticker

If Winston Churchill were a reader of today's newspapers, he might still have the same complaint. "Take back this newspaper, it has no theme. I'm too busy, I don't have time to search for what I need — don't they think I have more important things to do with my day? Can't they shed some light, not simply spread information? They call this color? The bloody thing is Pepto-Bismol pink. Grumble, harrumph! …"

A typical reader? Yes, according to readership studies conducted over the years by Chris Urban, president of Urban & Associates. She observes that because of years of conditioning and habit-building, readers have come to expect certain things from newspapers, among them: the news (obvious, but needs to top the list), accuracy, good editorial judgment, clarity, credibility, professionalism, consistency, and a respect for their time. In addition, readers suffer from sensory overload — too much to see and too much to hear. Finally, there is the conflict between readers' needs for continuity and for change.

Pressured by readers to change, many newspapers have turned to design to solve their problems. It doesn't. Graphic indulgences are not enough. However, if the design responds to readers' needs, it can advance our knowledge and ability to communicate more effectively. This means the designer/journalist must employ a variety of skills that combine intuition and intellect in order to address the complexity of the world being reported. He or she needs to communicate a more complete view and understanding of people and how they live.

Designing newspapers with such an approach is more like city planning than architecture. It requires not only management, editorial, and design insight, but also the ability to marshal the strategy required to redesign the organization. Such designs are attentive to the stake readers have in the newspaper, appropriate to the community served (the design operates in the context of the culture), and organized in a way that illuminates information with many points of entry for readers (◉4).

At the same time, the design is cohesive and gives readers a thread and internal logic they can follow with ease. It has a theme.

"Respecting readers' time takes many forms. It demands crisp, clear writing, of course, as well as treating page makeup and packaging as an inherent part of the communications process, and not just a cosmetic application after the fact."
Chris Urban
Market researcher

111

The newspaper
Connecting with today's readers

Our vision determines what we can achieve, so we should develop a strategy that encompasses a wide vista. In an effort to attract new readers, publishers — armed with marketing surveys and readership studies — analyze buying habits and redesign newspapers. This is not to say such studies aren't important. They are. They give essential information on which to base decisions. But a distinction should be made between two processes: the design process, which leads to discoveries, and the management process, which gathers and analyzes material. One process is organic and unpredictable and the other is mechanical and predictable. The folks who take the measure of the community and the newspaper may not be the ones best suited for exploration and creative discoveries.

In her book *The Writing Life,* Annie Dillard writes about the goals and intentions of the writer before putting pen to paper. She says that having a vision to write a book that will become a movie or the great American novel is not the same as following a creative process that can lead to discoveries. "What we aim for is what we can get, so we must be sure to aim for the right thing." In a section on "appealing workplaces," she tells of her need to chop wood to keep warm one winter in a cabin on an island in Puget Sound. She writes, "At first, in the good old days, I did not know how to split wood. I set a chunk of alder on the chopping block and harassed it, at enormous exertion, into tiny wedges that flew all over the sandflat and lost themselves. What I did was less like splitting wood than chipping flints. After a few whacks my alder chunk still stood serene and unmoved, its base untouched, its tip a thorn. ... One night, while all this had been going on, I had a dream in which I was given to understand, by the powers that be, how to split wood. You aim, said the dream — of course — at the chopping block, not at the wood; then you split the wood, instead of chipping it."

To try to attract readers by basing decisions only on what people buy is to aim at the wood, not the chopping block. Readers are more than the sum of what they buy. They stop reading newspapers not just because the content isn't there but also because it's too hard to extract. The real target then (the chopping block) is to improve the fundamental way in which we deliver information to readers through print.

Design explorations

These prototypes (left and right) attempt to discover new approaches to helping readers both receive *and* understand the news. Each makes use of devices such as a letter to readers from the editor putting the day's news in perspective, windows to the inside of the paper and to outside sources of information, and logos in headlines as primary signals.

With more effective communication you will reach not just one group — say a narrow target audience — but everyone.

This means delivering the news and helping readers navigate through it. Getting through a newspaper is much like traveling through a city. To get from here to there you need a road map. Along the way street signs direct and point to areas of interest. Readers welcome direction to help guide them through an ever-expanding wealth of information. With a good map and clear signs, they can set their speeds through pathways they've chosen.

A design that respects readers' time does three things: it organizes information, it uses visual signals to draw the reader to the information, and it packages the information for quick access.

The first step, organization, is achieved by creating an internal logic. This means finding a sequence and rhythm that makes sense.

113

The next step is to break down barriers to entry to the news by using visual signals, beacons that point beyond the surface of the page into the information itself.

These visual signals are successful only if used well. A lead paragraph can catch the reader's eye if it's set in 14-point type, but if it isn't gracefully written, if the type is not of good quality, and if the reproduction is poor, it's not effective communication.

Each visual signal has its own attribute, but all have one thing in common: They connect with the reader very quickly. Here are some signals I find useful as navigational aids for readers:

Logos identify a subject and create points of entry on a page.

Symbols add flavor to the facts and, like the U.S. flag, should be instantly recognizable.

Graphics can take readers where words and photos can't — into outer space or inside the earth.

Maps turn spaces into places, they organize and locate space, they connect readers to a place and point them to areas of interest.

At-a-glance boxes deliver salient facts quickly. They can be comparisons (candidates on the issues), chronologies (tracking the tragedy), highlights (key play of the game), profiles, or timelines.

Labels enable readers to find subjects they need. They are used in two ways: (1) to identify communities, such as the Bronx or Queens, and (2) to identify communities of interest, such as health or business.

Decks, used in combination with labels and headlines, give a lot of additional information quickly.

Chapter heads, replacing subheads, tell more and allow the reader to get into the story at critical points in the narrative. They require a process of editing that defines what's important in the story. A story on a treaty reducing missiles in Europe might be blocked with chapter heads announcing "The Battle," "The Provisions," "The Issues," "The Influential Voices," and "The Arsenals Eliminated under the Treaty."

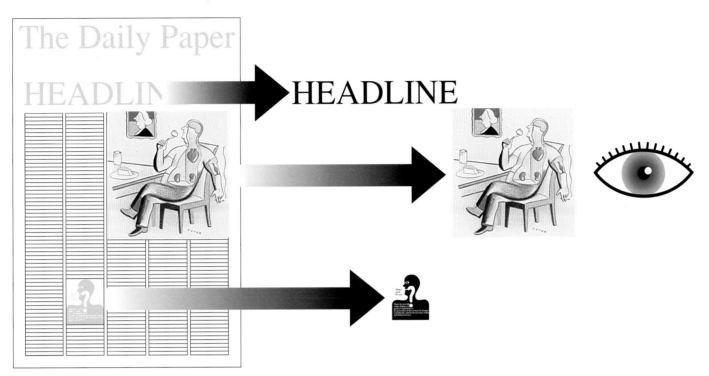

Freeze Frame

Illustration by Nigel Holmes

News rises up from the page to the eye at different speeds.

Color, graphics, headlines, and photos rise to the eye faster than text.

Summary paragraphs give the reader the essence of the story. Scanners get more out of a paper that uses summary paragraphs, and so do the deep-dippers who dive in.

Boldface nut graphs call attention to the flavor of the story.

Indexing, referring and creating windows to the inside, help guide readers to more information.

Color is like the human voice. It has volume as well as tone and pitch. Applying color to a page immediately turns up the volume, so it must be done well. A mediocre newspaper that suddenly adds color to its cheeks is still a mediocre newspaper.

Large text — using words as dominant graphic images — is another way of turning up the volume. After I had set a lead in 16-point type at *The Christian Science Monitor,* the editor had it rewritten because he thought it wasn't good enough for the larger display.

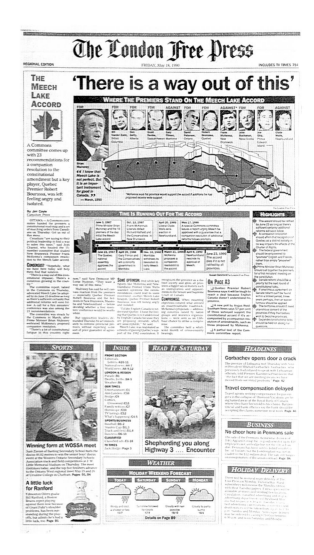

The third step in creating a design that respects readers' time is packaging.

Packaging stories in their appropriate form requires a process of editing that delivers not only narrative, but also explanatory pieces. It requires defining important news and giving it proper play. Here is an axiom you can depend on: Important stories should be longer and played well, unimportant stories shorter and packaged appropriately. Sometimes writers confuse length with depth. If all the stories are long and need to jump to inside pages, it shouldn't come as a surprise that readers become annoyed and impatient.

The challenge is to recognize which is which and let the content determine the length of the story and the shape it should take. Sig Gissler, editor of *The Milwaukee Journal,* put it this way: "Some stories are like flagpoles, others are like gear boxes. Take three feet off a

Packaging

Readers will seek editorial help to navigate through the ever-expanding amount of information. Simply announcing news events does not guarantee reader comprehension. As a result, packaging the information, making it comprehensive and comprehensible, will become even more essential. As seen in these Associated Press "Agenda 92" pages, it's an editing process in which we look for and discover themes that organize and make sense of the news (4).

flagpole, it's still a flagpole. Take anything out of a gear box and it won't work. Sorry," he would often tell a reporter," your story is a flagpole."

It's the same with layout. Stories can be thought of as text and laid out with length the primary consideration or as packages with each piece of information (text, photos, and graphics) an integral part of the whole. One approach stresses linear thinking, the other visual thinking.

As readers survey the newscape asking themselves where to invest their time, they look for information organized in a logical way, easy entry to that information, and intelligent packaging.

The Organization

For whom the bells toll

10 Guidelines

THE PROCESS OF CHANGING THE ORGANIZATION:

1. *Clearly state goals at the outset.*

2. *Break the organization down into its distinct parts and analyze those parts and how they are related.*

3. *Reassemble the different parts (for example, departments) and coordinate their activities to benefit the whole (not just the individual departments).*

4. *Create new realities as you proceed by institutionalizing new ideas and making clear to everyone the logic behind your ideas.*

Traditionally newspapers and newsrooms have been designed with a concern for enclosing space at as little cost per pica or per square foot as possible, rather than for the quality of the content or the space enclosed. Along the way we've paid scant attention to the intellectual and emotional impact of that content or those spaces on people who have to live with them. During the 1980s our cities changed noticeably as they adapted to expanding population growth and new economic realities. Under the banner of "the new," the revised look of a newspaper or a building frequently became a matter of fashion rather than style.

Skyscrapers are built in the latest fashion by architects with an axiom to grind rather than a concern for the fabric of the city. News pages stress design inventiveness rather than helping readers understand and find the content easily. To further complicate things, information — which formerly could be counted on to eliminate uncertainty — now increases people's feeling of insecurity.

To paraphrase Einstein: The Information Age has changed everything save our mode of thinking. We need to change our attitudes and think of ourselves as being in the information business as much as in the news business. With new ways of delivering information throughout the communications media, newspapers might continue to exist but could be forced out of their role as a mass medium. It doesn't have to be that way if journalists learn to think in new ways.

Look at interactive television. In January 1990 Tele-Metropole in Montreal broadcast the world's first interactive hockey game, a match between the Montreal Canadiens and the Quebec Nordiques. With interactive TV, viewers have a second remote control with one button that lets them replay whenever they want and two others that let them choose their own camera view. During a news program, for example, viewers can stop the news at any point and get a full report on that story, whether it's the crisis in Lithuania or the secession of the Maritime provinces. With such a black box, viewers can shop from their homes, access computer data banks, scan the day's news stories, or use a dozen other interactive TV services.

118

Since interactive TV gives viewers the power to choose camera shots and decide how much news they want, newspapers should be even more concerned with finding ways to help readers quickly get the information *they* want.

Look at the telephone company. It doesn't restrict its vision to phone consoles and the wires that connect them. It sees its role as a conveyor of information. The lines and equipment are a crucial part of that strategy, but hardly the only part. Computers, data, information services — these are the buzzwords of the modern telephone company.

Most newspaper organizations have not made that conceptual leap. They still see themselves in the business of putting ink on paper. The leap to the "information business" does not have to abandon publishing in the process, but it will help define the essential nature of what we should be selling: information packaged in a variety of ways that suit users.

Making the conceptual leap, however, doesn't guarantee that one can easily make the organizational leap. Many newspapers are hierarchical and rigid organizations bound by rules, procedures, and habits. By their nature such rigid structures tend to segregate and classify, compartmentalize and alienate, and confine individuals to mechanical and routine tasks. Until recently, the hierarchical model was thoughtlessly accepted as the only organizational model in the church, the military, and industry. There is nothing inherently wrong with this; it simply doesn't always work. As companies attempt to respond to the needs of the Information Age, they often turn to management solutions to nudge the organization forward when they can't reshape it totally. This was the case with the group of newspapers I worked on in Italy.

In 1986 I began the redesign of three newspapers in the Poligrafici group (☉ 74). The goal was to establish a core news operation in Bologna ("the information center") and then produce and electronically deliver national, sports, features, and business pages to newspapers in Florence, Trieste, and eventually Rome. Local news pages would be produced at each site. The assignment was to design pages that would be compatible with the technology and allow editors to insert important local news on their pages without reconfiguring the whole page. To do this we created a grid system built on modules or information blocks that became templates in the PC editorial system.

5. *Find ways to understand the value and true cost of each part and provide methods to improve quality and reduce costs.*

6. *Look for and find themes common to the village square and the global village.*

7. *Take thematic connections and see how they relate to the whole with an eye toward achieving specific goals.*

8. *Get people to discard old preconceptions.*

9. *Get people to embrace the same goals and speak the same language.*

10. *Create new models for the future. And remember, solutions that work should have no losers.*

*Before redesign,
divide and rule*

**The layout of the old newsroom
discouraged communication
between journalists. People were
boxed in and separated from one
another. Its form was ill-suited to
its purpose (◉ 20).**

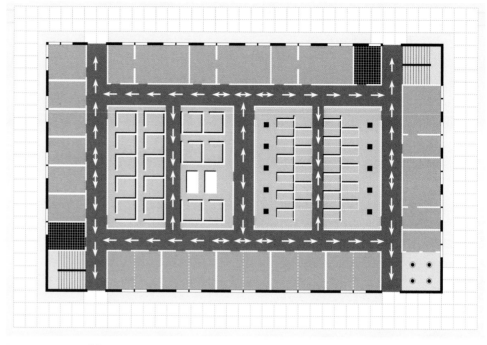

Mechanic *Closed plan*

Form = Substance

*Recognizing the effect
inherent formal
properties have on
people is the first step
toward creating
environments that
promote better
communication among
journalists, and in the
end, better newspapers.
Just as with the shape of
the newsroom, the shape
of the conference room
table can promote or
inhibit certain kinds of
discourse. The myth of
King Arthur and the
round table suggests that
a circular table is*

Trained as writers, not visual communicators, the journalists resisted
change of any kind. They approached their tasks with fixed attitudes,
mental preconceptions of how things ought to fit and function. Because
their conventional methods and formats led to predictable and dull
newspapers, the director created a separate agency to repackage the
information as special reports and graphics to be inserted into the core
paper or offered through other media. In the meantime, the introduction
of new PC-based technology is helping break down old, inflexible
structures and create newer, more democratic ones. There is an ancient
Roman saying: "The fates will lead him who will, the rest they drag."

There was similar resistance to change at *The London* (Ontario) *Free
Press* (◉ 94). The solution was to follow the rather radical redesign
effort with a two-year effort to redesign the newsroom. The project is
under way, and there is a willingness to try new approaches. One plan
envisions an open newsroom (see next page) with topic, or cluster,
groups — such as city, sports, business, environment, and health —
composed of teams of journalists, editors, writers, designers, and
photographers. A journalist can work on various teams with concern for
individual talent and skill rather than status or place on an
organizational chart.

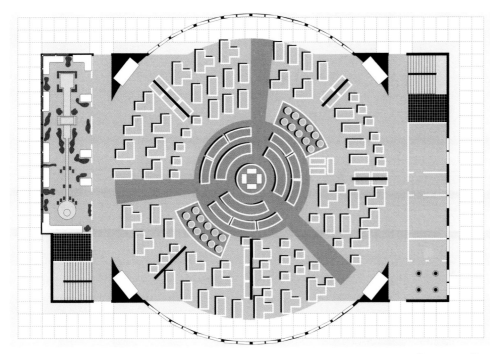

Organic *Open plan*

After redesign, democratizing the news operation

An integrated plan tailored for human interaction and ease of communication. This structure is better suited to produce the newspaper above (21).

Instead of the organizational image being the hierarchy, in the open plan (above) it resembles a web. The information flow is quicker because people aren't sequestered in compartments (offices). Because this plan has more pathways and connections than the closed plan, it allows people to communicate across traditional boundaries.

Pages are done on graphic workstations. Large computer screens positioned in the newsroom allow everyone to see section fronts as they are being developed. News meetings are divided into two formats: brainstorming and production. Special teams conceive and produce new products. Newsroom layout and new technologies are designed to support continuing efforts to democratize the newsroom and open the decision-making process to include more people.

In other words, an attempt is being made to redesign the newsroom in order to free journalists from the inhibiting structures of the past and to create an environment that admits the diversity and complexity of the world they are reporting. As we explore the newspaper of the '90s, the central question is not, "Will technology change?" (of course it will), but, "Will organizations and journalists change in appropriate ways?" (not necessarily).

more likely to promote good will and consensus than a rectangular one. The 16th-century English philosopher Francis Bacon observed: "A long Table, and a square Table, or seats about the walls seem Things of Forme, but are Things of Substance; for at a long Table, a few at the upper end, in effect, sway all the Businesse; but in the other Forme, there is more use of the Counsellours Opinions that sit lower."
R.L.

121

The journalist
It tolls for thee

"The only things which we commonly see are those which we pre-perceive, and the only things which we pre-perceive are those which have been labeled for us, and the labels stamped into our mind. If we lost our stock of labels we should be intellectually lost in the midst of the world."

William James

"On Preperception"

After redesigning the publisher and organization, the final step is to redesign the journalist. It comes as a shock to most journalists to discover that the automatic pilot of reactive thinking must be replaced by creative thinking in order to compete in today's world.

I've tried to demonstrate the link between staff organization and the resulting product — that we must create systems that are attuned to change. The task of managers should be to liberate people from the limits of structure. But after they are liberated, then what? Some journalists, vocationally trained, can deal with only part of the total communication process — words or pictures. Few have been educated to think visually *and* verbally (● 3).

In addition, some people in newsrooms frequently play "insider games": They set up barriers to keep outsiders (readers or other people in the organization) from knowing what's going on. The process is sovereign rather than democratic; it is exclusive rather than inclusive; it is "me" rather than "us." In such hierarchical systems, "truth" is the last word spoken by the highest-ranking person. Over the years these systems become more rigid and bound by rules, procedures, and habits. There emerges an artificial logic to things.

Furthermore, people tend to develop fixed attitudes, preconceived mental reactions that allow them to see and hear only what they expect to see and hear, thereby confirming their acquired beliefs. Pretty soon people are unable to step out of conventional ways of seeing and create one canon of journalism. Now if that canon is based on a narrow view of what newspapers should and can be — and it frequently is — they end up producing boring newspapers. In such cases they must change their way of thinking even though the forces against such change — a nostalgia for the past and the comfort of having things the way they've always been — are enormous.

In his book titled after the Frank Capra film *It's a Wonderful Life,* Stephen Jay Gould tells a story that illustrates how the discovery of an enormous number of fossils imprinted in the Burgess Shale followed this path. In 1909 Charles Doolittle Walcott, the longtime head of the Smithsonian Institution, first discovered the fossils and then proceeded to misclassify the thousands of fossils he had found. While reviewing and classifying the fossils, Walcott — mentally bound to a view of evolution as linear and progressive — decided without examining more deeply that they must be simple ancestors of the species we have on earth today. Gould observes that Walcott "shoehorns his specimens into the existing categories." The interpretation depended on the bias of the observer. His "mental template" permitted him to see what he expected to see and confirm his existing beliefs. He was wrong.

There is a myth about practitioners of journalism and science that they are objective observers and not affected by the same cultural biases that influence others. It's just as likely that "facts" are influenced by the preconceptions of these fact-finders. This is not a rallying cry for subjective journalism. It's a cautionary note that we engage in some personal scrutiny to identify our own biases in order to become as objective as possible.

For newspapers to survive and flourish in the future, journalists will have to broaden their communication and management skills as news organizations change their definition of what a newspaper is. The change requires a high degree of managerial, editorial, and design competence. It requires managers who can tolerate ideas other than their own, who can share authority, who can accept some degree of ambiguity in the chain of command, and who can champion teamwork. The most successful news pages are those produced by teams of journalists: editors, reporters, photographers, and artists. Too often we have people working on different sides of a newsroom fault line that divides "word people" from "picture people." This situation has led to one definition of print journalists as the "hunters and gatherers of the Information Age."

Many journalists *have* changed — from thinking in fragmented bits to the new integrated world of bits and bytes. Many newspapers now successfully integrate words, editing, and design. They focus on conveying information in an accessible way, realizing that a story is not simply text accompanied by some graphic device to relieve the grayness; rather, it is a package of information in which words and visual elements work together to transmit the message. And last but not least, by design many newspapers have become more attractive. After all, where beauty catches the eye, the mind follows.

Change

Writing to the poet Louise Bogan about the "severe strain" that their generation had undergone while continually adjusting to a world in flux, Edmund Wilson said, "Still we have to carry on. … The only thing that we can really make is our work. And deliberate work of the mind, imagination and hand … in the long run remakes the world."

Section five

News by design

All the king's horses and all the king's men

Form and purpose

"But we've always done it that way."

Back in the 1950s, when I was growing up in a small town in the mountains of Pennsylvania, people didn't think much about newspaper design. And there wasn't a lot of talk about the Age of Information either.

Society was simpler and so were newspapers. There was the women's page, with news of the comings and goings of prominent folks and what or who was showing in the local art league; the sports page, no agate but a lot of local stuff; and the news pages, the hard stuff, which were reserved for the front of the newspaper. And frequently that wasn't very interesting. If it was, it wasn't told in an interesting way. The idea that *how* you present information is as important as *what* you say had not yet reached newspapers. The tone of our local paper was gray. It was predictable. It was peaceful.

Newspapers are hardly peaceful places today. They have become battlegrounds in a struggle between the forces of change and those of the status quo.

Type cast

At the *Baltimore Sun*, Design Director Dick D'Agostino and I tried to create a look that reflected the special tone and character of the city. After the implementation of the redesign in 1984, Managing Editor Jim Houck wrote: "The design process has had a remarkable influence on the *Sun* — on the way we think about the newspaper and its relationship to its readers, on the way we think about the news, and in the way we present it."

127

Dear Readers

Readership studies often find readers who say, "What I need is to get an idea of the day's news while I have my morning cup of coffee." The common response to this has been the use of front-page briefs. Above are examples of a letter from the editor to the reader giving the highlights of the day's news.

At issue is whether newspapers will become lively and interesting with a greater diversity of information or continue to be produced as if being dull were a prerequisite for being taken seriously.

In the past decade newspaper design has become the primary battlefield in the war against dull, lifeless newspapers. Some editors have turned away from such ineffective communication. Much of what was wrong with newspapers, it seemed, was that many editors limited their options by what they thought news should be. They reduced the possibilities so much that many readers began to seek useful information elsewhere.

The complexity of news organizations makes them hard to manage. Even the way we conduct news meetings seems, almost by design, to filter out any trace of energy or vitality before the news hits the streets. From the management style of a newspaper you can predict the energy and excitement of the newspaper itself. The organizational structure can encourage or stifle creativity and enthusiasm. All human systems, especially newspapers, need to renew themselves periodically.

But both human and institutional resistance to change is great. There is a nostalgia for having things the way they always were. There develops a thought-police insistence that things remain the same. Relic specialists (curatorial figures who protect artifacts of the past) emerge and claim, "we can't change" because "there is only one true way of doing things." Or,

"we've always done it that way." They resist change because they think it will diminish their power.

Newspapers, however, have been changing in the most fundamental ways. They are changing their basic attitudes about what constitutes news and what kind of organization can best deliver it. Some newspaper organizations are becoming information centers; they view themselves in the business of selling information in many forms through different media.

Newspapers are being redesigned in response to readers' changing needs. That seems logical but, remember, it's only a recent development. Most are attempting to change and keep in step with the changes in the culture. At the same time, some are struggling not to be out of step with their communities as they recognize that indigenous designing is more responsive to the complex needs of readers.

The trend is irreversible. A new culture and a new information environment are emerging. And all the king's horses and all the king's men can't put the old environment back together again.

"People drive into the future looking in the rear-view mirror," Marshall McLuhan has said. They tend to use new technologies in the old form — aluminum siding on houses mimics clapboard, and plastic in automobiles simulates wood grain. I won't attempt to predict the

Tabloids
The 1983 Chicago *Sun-Times* redesign was an integral element in a two-year program of editorial enrichment. In Publisher James Hoge's words, "The goal was to broaden and deepen the *Sun-Times* in well-organized and lively ways. The paper, while strengthened in all areas of coverage, was to be easy to use and inviting to read."

Tabloids

Above are prototypes of tabloids in which the content suggests the look and feel of the redesign. In each paper the content was examined with an eye toward broadening the definition of what the news should be for its special audience.

future — which is simply the projection of a wish that things turn out according to our biases — but here are some interesting trends I think will continue to influence us:

Technology. Changes in technology seem to outpace our ability to know what those changes are. Technology, however, will continue to work in our favor in spite of ourselves. Most of the advances in computer technology that ignited the "electronic revolution" in newspaper publishing were not pioneered by publishers. Ours has been an industry rich in revenue and skimpy on R&D. That's beginning to change. Before we can change or redesign newspapers to respond to the technological challenges and opportunities this new age offers, we must first redesign the publishers who still see themselves in the business of printing ink on newsprint, not in the business of selling information at a profit. This requires taking a broader view of what the mission and methods of newspapers should be.

As the newspaper organization of today becomes the information center of tomorrow, we are gaining a clearer view of the link between the organizational structure and the resulting product. Existing technologies and those now visible on the horizon enable us to gather, store, process, and deliver information in a greater variety of ways. Telephones, facsimile machines, and personal computers have taken on a new

importance. The trend toward microcomputerization gives us greater control over the total product and permits us to search for and find the true value of doing business. Computers will not only continue to give us more sophisticated data-storing and data-dispensing capabilities, but also allow us to track each piece in the information-gathering process and tell us the cost along the way. A new information marketplace will emerge from the development of international computer highways, much like a national highway system for data. People will have access to computerized libraries the size of the Library of Congress.

On another level, advances in computer technology are helping to break down traditional barriers to cooperation between artist and editor (☉ 8). The "fault line" that once separated editors and artists is being replaced by a more integrated way of working. With PCs and software programs such as QuarkXPress, the ease with which pages can be designed and the ability to experiment with different versions — to see typefaces, images, and colors on the screen — free designers and editors to place more time and greater emphasis on the quality of assignments, editing, writing, and designing.

In addition, because of new technology, today's "production systems" will give way to interactive links with subscribers, many of whom will no longer have to wait at the front porch for the "daily paper."

Tabloids

Because tabloids can't be neatly divided into sections like broadsheets, greater effort is needed to highlight the day's top stories *and* help readers find information. The prototypes above designed in 1985 for the *Science Gazette* invite readers to the page and to interesting stories inside.

Technology

The redesign of *The Columbus Dispatch* included the introduction of Macintosh design stations in the art department and newsroom. Assistant Managing Editor Karl Kuntz led the technological effort to create a seamless link and to develop a color palette for the newspaper. Deadline color graphics and photos were in place before design implementation.

Staff. Designing the newspaper of the future begins with reshaping the journalist of the present (• 122). Newspapers produced by people trained in verbal skills who have not refined their visual thinking tend to end up as a mass of gray "content" decorated with some "art." Only when we realize that type can be art and art is the shape content takes can we present the news in a visually interesting way — in a way that first attracts the reader, then holds his or her attention while we tell our story. We need to invest more in our people (• 50). Few major industries spend as little on training and education of personnel as newspapers. Yet, demanding technologies and the challenges of others in the information business require constant education and reeducation.

Coverage. There will be more explanatory journalism with more aggressive assignments explaining complex local issues. Local stories getting the most attention will be stories on government and politics, the environment, health, energy, education, housing, consumer affairs, employment, justice, and transportation. More attention will be paid to the packaging and presentation of each story (• 116, 119). The collection and repackaging of data will become even more important because subscribers will be buying information in forms other than the daily newspaper.

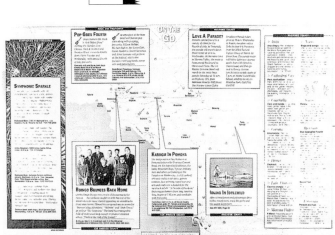

Editing. Editors will be highly skilled in more areas of communication. Visual and language skills will be part of their job requisites along with knowledge of management and technology. In a global society with instant information retrieval, readers will continue to seek human intervention to help navigate through the ever-expanding wealth of available data (⊙ 113). The existence of databases does not guarantee they'll be used or understood.

Writing. Writing styles will be tailored to the subject matter. For example, there will be the stripped-down, just-the-facts reporting of events, such as fires and crime stories. There will also be database sections (by phone or fax) devoted to statistical information, such as bank-by-bank interest rates and neighborhood crime statistics written in a functional style. A complex story explaining savings and loan abuses may be in question-and-answer form, anticipating reader questions and answering them. The poignant story of a family losing a baby to AIDS and how they cope with it may be told in a narrative style. At-a-glance boxes, written in a crisp, clear style, will be used to highlight salient facts in complex stories. All stories will have a tighter writing style. The worth of each word won't be devalued by continual overwriting in every part of the newspaper.

Indigenous designs

For a design to connect with the reader, it should be a good fit in the community. The history of the community and its special sense of place are essential elements in the design process (⊙ 31). Mel Opotowsky, senior managing editor of the *Press Enterprise*, led a two-year redesign effort that began with an analysis of the newspaper and the community to accomplish the goals of the redesign.

The regular Page A1 Digest is on Page A2 to accommodate today's expanded election coverage.

Due to expanded coverage of the NDP election victory, London and Region news is on Page A3 today.

Looking ahead

There are many stories that we can prepare for — stories with a long lifespan such as the war on drugs and the Gulf crisis and those with a shorter curve like sporting events or elections. The pages above were prepared and designed before the event. On the editorial side this means finding new ways of thinking about gathering and presenting information.

Design. There will continue to be more diversity in the look of newspapers. The design will be appropriate to the content and sensitive to the history of the area it serves.

Finally, while editors will still have the last word, they also will function in news environments in which journalists with intelligence, talent, imagination, and wit will participate in the decisions that affect their work and their readers' paper. The trend will continue toward management systems that are attuned to change and are sensitive to the individuals most affected by change, the readers.

Arnheim, Rudolf. *Art and Visual Perception.* Berkeley: University of California Press, 1967.

Arnheim, Rudolf. *Visual Thinking.* Berkeley: University of California Press, 1969.

Bronowski, J. *The Ascent of Man.* Boston: Little, Brown and Company, 1973.

Carpenter, Edmund. *Eskimo Realities.* New York: Holt, Rinehart and Winston, 1973.

Giedion, S. *The Beginnings of Architecture.* Princeton: Princeton University Press, 1964.

Holmes, Nigel. *Charts & Diagrams.* New York: Watson-Guptill Publications, 1984.

Kepes, Gyorgy. *Vision and Value Series.* New York: George Braziller, 1965.

McCoy, Katherine. "American Graphic Design Expression," *Design Quarterly 148* (1990).

Hurlburt, Allen. *The Grid.* New York: Van Nostrand Reinhold Company, 1978.

Kaufmann, Edgar, Jr. *Fallingwater.* New York: Abbeville Press Publishers, 1986.

Simonds, John Ormsbee. *Landscape Architecture.* New York: McGraw Hill Book Co. Inc. 1961.

Strunk, William, Jr., and E. B. White. *The Elements of Style.* 3d ed. New York: The Macmillan Company, 1979.

Wingler, Hans M. *The Bauhaus.* Cambridge: The MIT Press, 1969.

Dillard, Annie. *The Writing Life.* New York: Harper and Row, Publishers, 1989.

Gould, Stephen Jay. *Wonderful Life: The Burgess Shale and Nature of History.* New York: W. W. Norton, 1989.

Herdeg, Walter. *The Decorated Diagram.* Cambridge: The MIT Press, 1983.

Evans, Harold. *Editing and Design Series.* New York: Holt, Rinehart and Winston, 1974.

Finberg, Howard, and Itule, Bruce D. *Visual Editing.* California: Wadsworth Publishing Company, 1990.

Garcia, Mario R. *Contemporary Newpaper Design.* New Jersey: Prentice Hall, 1981.

Gerstner, Karl. *Compendium for Literates.* Cambridge: The MIT Press, 1974.

Safdie, Moshe. *Form and Purpose.* Aspen: International Design Education Foundation, 1980.

Visual thinking

Process

Art of change

News by design

135